STORIES AND SKETCHES OF OUR HYMNS AND THEIR WRITERS
HAZEL PARTRIDGE

ANNE ROSS COUSIN
Authoress of "The Sands of Time are Sinking"

Stories and Sketches of our Hymns and their Writers

DAVID J. BEATTIE

JOHN RITCHIE LTD
CHRISTIAN PUBLICATIONS

40 Beansburn, Kilmarnock, Scotland

ISBN-13: 978 1 909803 23 7

Copyright © 2013 by John Ritchie Ltd.
40 Beansburn, Kilmarnock, Scotland

www.ritchiechristianmedia.co.uk

All rights reserved. No part of this publication may be reproduced, stored in a retrievable system, or transmitted in any form or by any other means – electronic, mechanical, photocopy, recording or otherwise – without prior permission of the copyright owner.

Typeset by John Ritchie Ltd., Kilmarnock
Printed by Bell & Bain Ltd., Glasgow

Foreword.

THE singing of God's praises is clearly revealed in the Scriptures of truth as the Divine will for His people. "Singing and making melody with your heart to the Lord, in psalms and hymns and spiritual songs," is an injunction given to the churches (Eph. 5. 19, R.V.). Of Christ Himself it is said, "I will declare Thy Name unto My brethren: in the midst of the congregation will I praise Thee" (Psa. 22. 22 with Heb. 2. 12). His leading of praise in this manner is itself a token of the unity of Christ and His people, but, more than this, the song of the redeemed as led by Him will be the expression of His own infinite joy in the Church.

The Apostle Paul, in writing to the Church at Corinth, says, "I will sing with the spirit, and I will sing with the understanding also," using the first person in an exemplary and general way. Psalmody and later Hymnody became highly developed in the religious services of the Jews, and had a place in the Christian churches from the very beginning. In some of the later Epistles fragments of hymns appear to be quoted, as in Eph. 5. 14. The sentences of 1 Tim. 3. 16 constitute a stanza, and were probably a recognized confession set in the form of a hymn.

Tertullian mentions that at the love-feasts, after water was furnished for the hands and the lights were lit, friends were invited to sing praises to God either from Scripture or by way of improvised compositions. Pliny records how Christians used to gather together even before daylight to sing hymns to Christ in alternating responses.

Foreword—Continued.

Provision for such praise has been abundantly made by God, through the guidance of the Holy Spirit, right through the present age, as witnessed by the great number of hymns and spiritual songs written in the choicest language, for the use of His people individually and collectively. It was therefore a happy idea which occurred to the author of the present Volume to make a compilation of stories and sketches of our hymns and their writers.

The hymns which direct the heart immediately to the worship of God and to heart occupation with the Father and with His Son Jesus Christ our Lord are of pre-eminent value in the realm of spiritual hymnody. The author has appropriately chosen the story of T. Kelly for a first place in the book; for a large number of the 700 hymns written by him are of the character to which reference has just been made, though many of the hymns written by others whose lives are under review, are of an equally deep-toned worship to the Lord.

It has perhaps not been sufficiently considered what a very important service Divinely helped hymn-writers have rendered, both to individuals and to the churches. It is quite usual for us, generally speaking, to make use of hymns while knowing scarcely anything, or even nothing at all, of the servants of God who wrote them. The narratives and details of the following pages helpfully supply what has been lacking in this respect. The work accomplished by Mr. D. J. Beattie gives evidence of careful research on his part and of the devotion of much time and toil involved in the preparation of such a Volume.

The kind request made by the author as to the writing of this Foreword, when yet the book was in its early stages, has made the acceptance to do

Foreword—Continued.

so, on the part of the writer, an even greater pleasure and privilege after pursuing the proofs in their final form. His earnest desire is that the book may have an extensive circulation, and that it may be abundantly owned of God for the edification and refreshment of the souls of the readers.

Bath, June, 1934.   W. E. VINE.

Contents.

	Page
Thomas Kelly	9
Sir Edward Denny	13
John Nelson Darby	17
James G. Deck	21
Samuel Medley	24
Robert Robinson	27
Isaac Watts	29
Augustus M. Toplady	34
Charles Wesley	36
William Cowper	38
John Newton	42
Philip Dodridge	46
William Williams	48
James Montgomery	51
John Bakewell	55
Thomas Olivers	56
R. M. McCheyne	59
Joseph Hart	63
Robert Hawker	65
John Fawcett	67
Walter Shirley	68
John Cennick	69
John Mason	70
Joseph Scriven	72
Hugh Stowell	75
Samuel P. Tregelles	77
Thomas R. Taylor	80
Horatius Bonar	82
Robert C. Chapman	86
J. Denham Smith	90
S. Trevor Francis	94
Edward H. Bickersteth	98
Henry F. Lyte	100
Reginald Heber	102
Albert Midlane	104
Alexander Steward	108
James G. Small	111
George Matheson	113
Josiah Conder	115
Bernard Barton	117
James H. Evans	118
Ernst C. Homburg	120
Joseph Swain	121
Frederick Whitfield	123

	Page
Andreas Bernstein	125
James Hutton	126
George Keith	128
John Berridge	129
John Withy	132
George Burder	133
James Boden	135
William Reid	137
William P. Mackay	140
Douglas Russell	143
Philip P. Bliss	148
H. G. Spafford	151
Daniel W. Whittle	153
James McGranahan	156
H. Grattan Guinness	158
Edward Mote	162
W. O. Cushing	164
Edgar P. Stites	165
J. H. Gilmore	167
Robert Lowry	168
Edward P. Hammond	170

Lady Hymn Writers.

F. R. Havergal	172
Fanny Crosby	176
Mary J. Walker	180
Anne Steele	183
Charlotte Elliott	185
Margaret L. Carson	188
Elizabeth Codner	189
Mary Peters	192
Jane Crewdson	193
Mary Shekleton	195
Anne R. Cousin	196
Marianne Nunn	200
Jane E. Leeson	201
Jane E. Hall	202
Amelia M. Hull	202
Lady Campbell	203
Charitie L. Bancroft	204
Elizabeth C.D.Clephane	205
Hannah K. Burlingham	207
Frances Bevan	210

Stories and Sketches
OF OUR
Hymns and their Writers.

◆

THOMAS KELLY.

Praise the Saviour, ye who know Him!
Who can tell how much we owe Him?
Gladly let us render to Him
    All we are and have.

HOW many sweet memories circle round this exultant hymn of praise, carrying our thoughts back to the days of our first love, then onward through life, singing itself into almost every phase of our Christian pilgrimage journey. Wedded to "Orphrah," a simple but singularly pleasing tune, it is a hymn that at once fixes itself on the believer's mind and heart, ready to burst forth at the first note of praise.

Thomas Kelly, the author, was born in Dublin in 1769. He was the son of an Irish judge, and it had been young Kelly's intention to follow the career of his father. With this purpose in view, after graduating with honours at Trinity College, Dublin, he entered the Temple in London, but having undergone a great spiritual change through an earnest study of the Scriptures, he renounced the law as a profession and returned to Dublin where, at the age of twenty-three, he became a minister of the Established Church.

Kelly was too evangelical, however, for the Archbishop of Dublin of that day, and with his friend Rowland Hill, was inhibited from preaching in the diocese. This led Kelly to associate himself with those believers who were faithful to the teaching of God's Word and the spreading of the glorious Gospel. Being possessed of ample means, he built places of worship at Athy, Portarlington, Wexford, and other towns in the neighbourhood, where he preached to large gatherings, gradually rallying round him a strong evangelical party. He was an eloquent speaker, and being endowed with wonderfully magnetic powers, Mr. Kelly attracted great crowds to hear him.

As a hymn writer he possessed a prolific pen, and altogether over 700 hymns were written by him, a great number of which are in general use to-day.

Kelly was also a composer of considerable ability, and many of his hymns were first set to music by the author himself. Unlike present-day hymn books with words and music conveniently set together, it was necessary for the worthy leader of praise of that day to carry with him to worship the familiar tune book. Soon after the publication of his collection of hymns in 1815, Mr. Kelly issued a companion volume containing tunes suited to the various metres found in his hymn book.

Thomas Kelly's ever-living influence will illustrate his own happy saying. Lord Plunkett, an old school-fellow of his, met him one day in later life, and said, "You will live to a great age, Mr. Kelly!" "Yes," was the ready reply, "I am confident I shall, as I expect never to die!" Of a charitable and kindly disposition, Mr. Kelly was beloved by all with whom he came in contact. Especially was this the case among the poor of Dublin. A story is told

HYMNS AND THEIR WRITERS.

of a worthy old couple who were passing through a time of great poverty and distress. The husband had much difficulty in keeping up the drooping spirits of his wife. "Bridget," said he one day, "hould up, my lass, there's always Misther Kelly to pull us out of the bog after we've sunk for the last time."

It is said that no really deserving case appealed to him in vain, and the memory of good Mr. Kelly was cherished by the poor of the Irish Capital long after he had gone home to his reward.

The compositions of Kelly are marked by their power and outstanding beauty. A hymn first published in 1809, and to-day in popular and extensive use both in Great Britain and America, is the one commencing:—

> Look, ye saints, the sight is glorious;
> See the 'Man of Sorrows' now!
> From the fight returned victorious:
> Every knee to Him shall bow!
> Crown Him! Crown Him!
> Crowns become the Victor's brow.

As an indication of the favour extended to the hymns of Thomas Kelly, obviously because of their distinct usefulness, it is worthy of note that three of the best known† hymn books in use amongst Open Brethren, so-called, each contains a percentage of his compositions perhaps greater than that of any other hymn writer. Of that number reference is here made to the following which are especially familiar—

> We'll sing of the Shepherd that died,
> That died for the sake of the flock.

There is that grand exultant song—

> Praise the Lord who died to save us,
> Praise His ever gracious name.

† "Believers Hymn Book," "Hymns for Christian Worship," "Hymns of Light and Love."

Then we have that sweet hymn so often sung—

> The atoning work is done,
> The Victim's blood is shed.

Also that exquisitely beautiful hymn—

> Behold the Lamb with glory crowned,
> To Him all power is given.

And that choice hymn, fragrant with sweet memories—

> The head that once was crowned with thorns
> Is crowned with glory now;
> A royal diadem adorns
> The mighty Victor's brow.

In the preface of the last edition of his hymns, published in 1853, Mr. Kelly gives this interesting and beautiful personal testimony, eminently characteristic of his unfailing faith:—

> It will be perceived by those who may read these hymns, that though there is an interval between the first and the last of near sixty years, both speak of the same great truths, and in the same way. In the course of that long period, the author has seen much and heard much; but nothing that he has seen or heard has made the least change in his mind, that he is conscious of, as to the grand truths of the Gospel. What pacified the conscience then does so now. What gave hope then does so now. 'Other foundation can no man lay than that is laid, which is Christ Jesus.'

Many of Kelly's hymns are of exceptional merit and rank with the first in the English language. He passed to be with Him of Whom he never ceased to sing, in 1854, at the advanced age of eighty-five.

SIR EDWARD DENNY.

> Sweet feast of love Divine!
> 'Tis grace that makes us free,
> To feed upon this bread and wine,
> In memory, Lord, of Thee.

PRECIOUS indeed are these familiar lines to many of us; and how often the heart, in some passing moment, is unconsciously prompted to song, at the sweet remembrance of its theme. To the toiler, as he bends to his weary task, and to the patient mother, as she lulls to sleep the babe upon her breast, the hymn is indeed a well of consolation, which, in thought, transports the child of God from the transient scenes of earth, to the sweetest and most precious of all joys to be found around the Lord's table.

Sir Edward Denny, fourth baronet of Tralee Castle, County Kerry, who gave to us this beautiful communion hymn, was born on the 2nd October, 1796, and succeeded his father in August, 1831.

Though born in high degree, with its many advantages of wealth and environment, Sir Edward was early drawn aside from the world's swift-flowing current, in a remarkable way, by the reading of "Father Clement." Pointing to the book one day, when in his ninetieth year, he remarked to a friend who sat with him in his library at West Brompton, that under God, to it he owed his conversion. He resided much in London, and for some considerable time was closely connected with Park Walk Assembly, where his ministry, given in a quiet and unassuming way, was always appreciated. Sir Edward was a writer of some ability, many of his prose contributions being in prophetic vein. It is, however, as a hymn writer that the name of Sir Edward Denny will always be remembered. His first publication, "A selection of Hymns," appeared in 1839, which was followed, a few years later, by "Hymns and Poems." In his introduction to this collection, the author, referring to 1 Corinthians 13. writes: "Love, then, as we read, being 'the greatest of these,' seeing that the blessed God is Himself essentially Love, our hopes should not surely come short of that day when He Whom, not having seen, we love, will reveal Himself to our hearts in all His attractions; when our powers of loving will be fully developed. And this will not be till the whole family meet in the house of their Father; till the Bride, the Lamb's Wife, is actually enthroned with her Lord. 'Come, Lord Jesus!'"

Many of Sir Edward's hymns are in extensive use both in this country and America, the most familiar being found in the hymn books already referred to, which are in use amongst the various assemblies throughout the United Kingdom. Sweetest and most loved of all his compositions is the hymn:

> To Calvary, Lord! in spirit now,
> Our weary souls repair,
> To dwell upon Thy dying love,
> And taste its sweetness there.

At the first note of that plaintive meditation hymn, are not our thoughts wafted to that sacred scene on the "green hill far away?"—that scene for ever precious to the child of God:—

> Sweet resting-place of every heart
> That feels the plague of sin,
> Yet knows the deep, mysterious joy
> Of peace with God within!

SIR EDWARD DENNY

Another of Sir Edward's hymns of almost equal merit with the preceding one, begins:

> 'Tis past the dark and dreary night,
> And, Lord, we hail Thee now—
> Our Morning Star, without a cloud
> Of sadness on Thy brow.

The fourth verse is marked by a pathos with which many of his compositions are characterised:

> Drawn from Thy pierced and bleeding side,
> That pure and cleansing flood
> Speaks peace to every heart that knows
> The virtues of Thy blood.

Many a beautiful hymn has been ruined by an inappropriate or ill-chosen tune. This, however, cannot be said in the present instance. "Harrington," the melody to which " 'Tis past the dark and dreary night" is set, and with which we are most familiar, is both pleasing and appropriate, and eminently suited to the words.

Other well-known hymns by the same author, are: "Bright with all His crowns of glory," "A pilgrim through this lonely world," "Bride of the Lamb, rejoice, rejoice," "What grace, O Lord, and beauty shone," "While in sweet communion feeding," and that hymn full of hope and consolation:

> O what a lonely path were ours,
> Could we, O Father, see
> No home or rest beyond it all,
> No guide or help in Thee.
>
> Sweet hope! we leave without a sigh
> A blighted world like this,
> To bear the cross, despise the shame,
> For all that weight of bliss.

Sir Edward Denny passed away in June, 1889, at the ripe age of ninety-three. By his tenantry he was held in the highest respect, his many kindly actions proving him to be an exceedingly lenient and considerate landlord. A very palpable evidence of the relationship that existed between him and the tenants on his estate, is shown in the following interesting notice which appeared in the press at the time of his death:

> "Nearly the whole town of Tralee belonged to him. He had an opportunity twenty years ago, when his leases fell in, of raising his rents to figures that, in some cases, would not have been considered extortionate had they been quadrupled. He, however, decided to accept the old rates. The result was that he was almost alone in escaping any reduction at the hands of the Land Commission. So far as he himself was concerned, a little money went a long way, but he gave liberally to poor relations, and to the development of religious work in connection with the Brethren. Living in a quiet way in a cottage at Islington, he devoted his time to the study of the prophetic books. His rental income from Ireland was about £13,000 a year."

The hymns and writings of Sir Edward Denny reveal the true meditative spirit of the writer, unmistakeably demonstrated in the closing stanza of the hymn with which this chapter opens:

> Thy sympathies and hopes are ours,
> We long, O Lord, to see
> Creation, all—below, above—
> Redeem'd and bless'd by Thee.

J. N. DARBY.

O Lord, Thy love's unbounded!
So sweet, so full, so free!
My soul is all transported,
Whene'er I think on Thee.

Yet, Lord, alas! what weakness
Within myself I find;
No infant's changing pleasure
Is like my wandering mind.

FEW hymns have been written which breathe in language so profoundly expressive, the unchanging love of God, than the inspiring lines by John Nelson Darby, of which the opening stanza is given. The author, whose name to-day, in Brethren circles, is a household word, was the youngest son of John Darby of Leap Castle, King's County, Ireland. Born at Westminster on November 18th, 1800, he was educated at Trinity College, Dublin, where he graduated in 1819, and in due course was called to the Bar. He subsequently became a high church clergyman, and was appointed by Archbishop Magee to the Wicklow parish of Calary, where he took up residence in the humble dwelling of a poor peasant on the bog side.

A man of outstanding personality, he made a deep and lasting impression on the simple country folk under his charge. It was about this time that he was introduced by J. G. Bellett to several friends, whose names in years to come were to be so closely associated with a world-wide movement, which had its origin in small and unpretentious gatherings in Dublin. In 1828, Mr. Darby resigned his curacy and severed his connection with the State Church by throwing in his lot with the few believers who had come together to "break bread."

It may seem superfluous to state that the name "Plymouth Brethren" is a misnomer, for as we have seen, the first gathering took place in the Irish Capital, the regular meeting subsequently being held in the premises of an auctioneer, in Aungier Street, hired by Mr. Parnell (afterwards Lord Congleton) in 1830. The most prominent names of those who took the step which was willed of God to become historic, were, Anthony Norris Groves, J. G. Bellett, John Parnell, Dr. Cronin and J. N. Darby.

The passing of a century has wrought many changes since the bond of fellowship linked together the little company, which has extended to the five continents of the world. This phenominal development was in a great measure due to the indefatigable efforts of J. N. Darby.

Amongst those with whom he came in contact during his scholastic career were W. E. Gladstone, a future Prime Minister of Great Britain, and Francis William, brother of J. H. Newman, who afterwards wrote the famous hymn "Lead kindly light." Attracted by the great personality of Darby, Newman invited him to visit Oxford, where he was introduced to B. W. Newton. "Newton, who was a native of Plymouth," says a contemporary, "brought about a visit by Darby to that town, strongly evangelical through the ministry of Dr. Hawker, and influenced by the 'separation' principles of John Walker, another Irish ex-clergyman. By the year 1832, a 'gathering' of believers 'to the name of Jesus,' the first of its order in England, was definitely formed there. James L. Harris, resigning his local incumbency of Plymstock, united with the Brethren, and started their first organ, 'The Christian Witness,' to which J. N. Darby contributed. S. P.

HYMNS AND THEIR WRITERS. 19

Tregelles, the textual critic, who was Newman's brother-in-law, was 'received' in 1836; after R. C. Chapman, at Barnstaple, and H. Craik with G. Muller, at Bristol, had taken like position. Great simplicity and devotedness marked the company in those golden days."

Darby travelled in many countries of Europe, also visiting America, the West-Indies, and New Zealand, ministering the Word and founding gatherings of Christians, who rejoiced in the wonderful truths he revealed to them from the Word of God. He devoted with untiring energy, the greater part of a long and busy life to the exposition of the Scriptures; his "Synopsis of Books of the Bible" is his lasting monument.

Though J. N. Darby ranks among our own hymn writers and receives a prominent position in "Julian's Dictionary of Hymnology," yet his name is remembered mainly as a Bible expositor rather than a writer of hymns. His hymns are comparatively few in number, but as might be expected from a theologian of the calibre of J. N. Darby, the verses from his pen are profoundly expressed, and throb with spiritual life.

"O Lord, Thy love's unbounded," written while the author was travelling on the top of a stage-coach, is one of his best hymns, and was first published in 1848. Another from his pen appearing at the same time, is still in use:

> This world is a wilderness wide—
> I've nothing to seek or to choose;
> I've no thought in the waste to abide;
> I've nought to regret or to loose.

It is said that Darby received the inspiration to write this hymn when on a visit to Killarney in Ireland.

Among his earliest compositions, which appeared in the year 1837 in "Hymns for the Poor of the Flock"—one of the first hymnal collections used amongst Brethren—is a spirited song of praise, commencing:

> Hark! ten thousand voices crying,
>   'Lamb of God!' with one accord;
> Thousand, thousand saints replying,
>   Wake at once the echoing chord.
>
> 'Praise the Lamb,' the chorus waking,
>   All in heaven together throng,
> Loud and far, each tongue partaking,
>   Rolls along the endless song.

Another hymn written about this time, which, along with the hymns already referred to, have appeared in various collections used in connection with assemblies of the Lord's people, is still a favourite:

> Rise, my soul, thy God directs thee;
>   Stranger hands no more impede;
> Pass thou on; His hand protects thee,
>   Strength that has the captive freed.

This hymn was written in Switzerland when a large number of Christians left the Swiss Free Church ("L'Englise Libre"), after some lectures given by Mr. Darby on The Book of Exodus. It was first published in "The Christian Hymn Book" in 1837.

The evening of a strenuous life was spent at Bournemouth, where, on April 29th, 1882, John Nelson Darby, one of the stalwarts of these last days, passed away in his eighty-second year.

J. G. DECK.

> Lord Jesus! are we one with Thee?
> O height, O depth of love!
> Once slain for us upon the tree,
> We're one with Thee above.

JAMES GEORGE DECK, the writer of this hymn was born at Bury St Edmunds, on November 1st, 1807. Choosing the army as a profession he studied at Paris under one of Napoleon's generals, and at the age of seventeen went to India as an officer, having received a commission in the 14th Madras Native Infantry. Young Deck had not been long abroad till he became deeply convicted of sin, and on one occasion in his sincerity for a better life, he drew up a code of resolutions, which he signed with his own blood, only to find himself without strength to keep them. In this unhappy state he continued for two years, when he returned to England on furlough in 1826. But the young officer had a praying mother "who used to retire every evening to her room for a quiet hour with God, on behalf of her children." Coming under the sweet influence to be found in the old home circle, he threw aside his resolutions, and

> Cast his deadly 'doing' down—
> Down at Jesus' feet.

Returning to India he boldly witnessed for Christ amongst his brother officers, a number being led to the Saviour through his instrumentality. In 1835 he resigned his commission, and returned home with the intention of becoming a clergyman in the Church of England. With this object in view he made a diligent study of the Scriptures, but being unable to see the will of the Lord in taking such a step, Mr. Deck sought special guidance, and was led to associate himself with a number of Christians who have since become known as "Brethren." Full of zeal for the Master, he now began to devote his energies in the preaching of the Gospel, his sphere of labour being the villages of Devon, where many precious souls were won for the Saviour. But the name of J. G. Deck will be better known to posterity by the many beautiful hymns he wrote rather than as a Gospel preacher.

It was in the year 1838 that he wrote that sweet adoration hymn, beginning:—

> Lamb of God! our souls adore Thee
> While upon Thy face we gaze;
> There the Father's love and glory
> Shine in all their brightest rays;
> Thine Almighty power and wisdom
> All creation's works proclaim;
> Heaven and earth alike confess Thee,
> As the ever great 'I AM.

To the believer there is an immeasurable depth of beauty in these lines, ever reminiscent of precious moments spent in His presence.

Another hymn written about the same time is one full of joyous anticipation of the Lord's coming again:—

> A little while! Our Lord shall come,
> 'And we shall wander here no more;
> He'll take us to our Father's home
> Where He for us has gone before;
> To dwell with Him, to see His face,
> And sing the glories of His grace.

J. G. Deck is also the author of "O Lamb of God still keep us," "O Lord, when we Thy path retrace," "The veil is rent! Lo, Jesus stands!" "O happy day when first we felt," and that hymn so much beloved:—

JAMES GEORGE DECK.

> Lord, we would ne'er forget Thy love,
> Who has redeemed us by Thy blood;
> And now, as our High Priest above,
> Dost intercede for us with God.

For some years Mr. Deck moved about amongst small gatherings of believers in the South Western Counties of England, being much used in establishing those who believed in the divine truths and principles which in God's Word had become so precious to himself.

A severe illness in 1852 compelled Mr. Deck to give up all thought of further ministry, and in accordance with medical advice he decided to emigrate to New Zealand. Mr. Deck settled near the village of Motueka, in Nelson province, where not many months after their arrival he suffered the loss of his devoted wife. In course of time, his health having been greatly restored, Mr. Deck with his family removed in 1865 to Wellington, where he spent many happy years ministering to the various assemblies in the province. Later, he returned with his family to their old home at Motueka, where, after a useful life, the greater part of which was faithfully devoted to the Lord's Work, J. G. Deck was called home on 14th August, 1884, in his 76th year.

From both a spiritual and literary standpoint, the compositions of J. G. Deck show high excellence, and are marked by an expressive tenderness which pervades many of them. His hymns were first published in "Hymns for the Poor of the Flock," in 1837; and were subsequently used in his brother-in-law's (Dr. Walker's) "Psalms and Hymns," in 1855. Mr. Deck's sister, Mrs. Mary J. Walker, is the authoress of several well-known hymns, including "Jesus I will trust Thee."

SAMUEL MEDLEY.

> Now in a song of grateful praise
> To Christ my Lord my voice I'll raise;
> With all His saints I'll join to tell,
> My Jesus has done all things well.

SAMUEL MEDLEY, the author of this old favourite and many other hymns in general use to-day, was born on June 23rd, 1738, at Cheshunt, Herts., where his father kept a school. He received a good education, and on leaving school was apprenticed to a business of his father's choice, but having a longing for the sea, the boy left his employment and entered the Royal Navy. He saw some active service, and was severely wounded in a battle with the French fleet, off Port Lagos, in 1759, after which he retired to civil life.

Samuel Medley lived in the days of four pioneers of English hymnody. He was ten years old when Isaac Watts, the father of English hymnody died. It is a remarkable circumstance that it was a sermon by Dr. Watts, read to Medley when he was a young man of twenty-two, that led to his conversion. He lived during the lifetime of Philip Doddridge, the writer of "Grace 'tis a charming sound," and John Newton, the author of "How sweet the name of Jesus sounds"; whilst James Montgomery, who wrote "For ever with the Lord," was a young man when Samuel Medley died.

Thus he was reared in an atmosphere when the use of hymns in public and private worship was beginning to make itself felt in England. It may possibly have been this circumstance that inspired him to direct his talent of verse-writing into a channel of usefulness, to be owned of God in

HYMNS AND THEIR WRITERS. 25

years to come. Soon after his conversion he actively associated himself in the Lord's work, and became identified with the Baptist Church in Eagle Street, London, then under the care of Dr. Gifford. He shortly afterwards opened a school, which for a number of years he conducted with remarkable success, employing his spare time in the preaching of the Gospel. Before he had reached his thirtieth year, Mr. Medley received a call to become pastor of the Baptist church at Watford. Five years later, in 1772, he removed to Byrom Street, Liverpool, where, as a result of his faithful ministry and fearless declaration of the Gospel, he gathered together a large and influential congregation. Here he laboured with untiring zeal for twenty-seven years, and passed away on July 17th, 1799.

It was during his ministry at Liverpool that the greater number of his hymns were written. These were first issued on broadsheets which were afterwards collected into a volume. Since then, Medley's hymns have been included in a considerable number of hymnals, particularly those of his own denomination and kindred gatherings of the Lord's people. Among his best known hymns is the one beginning:

> Awake, my soul, in joyful lays,
> And sing my great Redeemer's praise;
> He justly claims a song from thee;
> His loving-kindness—Oh, how free!
>
> He saw me ruined in the fall,
> Yet loved me notwithstanding all;
> He saved me from my lost estate;
> His loving-kindness—Oh, how great!

This hymn was the work of a few moments. Samuel Medley was visiting some friends in London, when, turning to the young daughter of his host he said—"Betsy, will you bring me some paper and ink?" On receiving the writing material he retired to an adjoining room, and after a comparatively short absence, returned with the whole of the hymn, almost as it appears to-day.

The Betsy referred to was born in 1783, became Mrs. Dodds, and died in America in 1861. These particulars, according to Mr. S. W. Duffield, a hymnal authority, came from her lips, through relatives residing in Washington.

The hymns of Samuel Medley, though their charm consists less in poetical form than in the warmth with which they give expression to Christian experience, have received no small measure of popularity since their birth over a hundred years ago. The hymn books already referred to have been happy in their choice of Medley's hymns taken from among his best compositions. Besides the two hymns quoted, the following are familiar: "The Saviour lives, no more to die," "On Christ salvation rests secure," and his triumphant song of praise:

> Come, let us sing the matchless worth,
> And sweetly sound the glories forth,
>   Which in the Saviour shine:
> To God and Christ our praises bring;
> The song with which the heavens ring,
>   Now let us gladly join.

ROBERT ROBINSON.

LIVING about this time was another hymn writer who is remembered by a single composition. His name was Robert Robinson, and the hymn which gave him a place on the roll of English hymn writers is one of surpassing beauty:

> Come, thou Fount of every blessing,
> Tune my heart to sing Thy grace;
> Streams of mercy never ceasing,
> Call for songs of loudest praise.

It was written about the year 1758. The authorship was for many years claimed for the Countess of Huntingdon, but the discovery of evidence in the author's own handwriting, proved conclusively that the hymn was the composition of Robinson.

There is an interesting story relating to this hymn. In the coaching days of long ago, a lady was seated on the outside of a stage-coach reading. During the journey, she had been intently engaged over one particular page of a little book which she consulted from time to time, with evident enjoyment. Turning to her fellow passenger, she held the open page towards him, and pointing to the hymn she had been reading, asked his opinion of it. The gentleman glanced at the first few lines but read no further, and turning away, evaded the question, endeavouring to direct the lady's attention to some other topic. She, however, again approached the subject, telling her fellow traveller of the wonderful blessing she had derived from the hymn, and expressing her great admiration of its sentiments. For a time the stranger appeared unmoved by the lady's appeal, till at length, overcome beyond the power of controlling his feelings, he burst into tears. "Madam," he said, "I am the poor unhappy man who wrote that hymn many years ago, and I would give a thousand worlds, if I possessed them, to enjoy the feelings I then had." The stranger was none other than Robert Robinson, who, sad to relate, had left the joy of his first love and drifted back into the world. Brought up in humble circumstances, Robinson, when a lad, was sent by his widowed mother to London, where he was apprenticed to a barber. Coming under the influence of Whitefield, the eminent preacher, the young man was converted to God, and soon after began to study the Scriptures with a view to becoming a preacher. At the age of twenty-five, Robinson was called to the pastorate of the Baptist Church of Cambridge. As already stated, poor Robinson, in later years, wandered away from God, and lapsed into sinful ways. He died suddenly on June 9th, 1790. When we remember the sad shipwreck of a useful life, there is a pathos in the lines he once wrote—

> Oh, to grace how great a debtor
> Daily I'm constrained to be;
> Let that grace, Lord, like a fetter,
> Bind my wandering heart to Thee.
>
> Prone to wander, Lord, I feel it;
> Prone to leave the God I love;
> Here's my heart, oh, take and seal it,
> Seal it for Thy courts above.

ISAAC WATTS.

> When I survey the wondrous cross
> On which the Prince of Glory died,
> My richest gain I count but loss,
> And pour contempt on all my pride.

ISAAC WATTS, the author of this universally loved hymn, is rightly regarded as the founder of English hymnody. Before his time, only a very few hymns, which were supplemented by crude versions of the Psalms, were sung in public worship. His father was the Deacon of a Congregational Chapel at Southampton, and young Isaac, who regularly attended the services, persistently complained to him of the indifferent quality of the hymns and Psalms which were then in use.

"Then give us something better, young man," was his father's curt reply. The young man determined to do so, and the following Sunday arrived with his first hymn. It was so favourably received that he was requested to write another. Thus began the reputation as a hymn writer of one whose songs of Zion are, to-day, sung throughout Christendom.

Isaac Watts was born on July 17th, 1674, at Southampton, where his father kept a boarding-school. Those were the days of early nonconformity, when religious zeal ran high, and young Isaac, on more than one occasion witnessed the imprisonment of his father, who, because of his settled religious convictions, was seized in his home and thrown into prison. Of a studious nature, Watts at an early age gave evidence of a desire to enter the ministry, and after fulfilling the position of tutor in the family of a county gentleman, he eventually became pastor of the famous Independent congregation in Mark Lane, London. Up to this time, while prosecuting his studies, Watts had been busy with pen and notebook, and many of his hymns were written around that period. Never very robust in constitution, the strain brought on by his strenuous work began to make itself evident, and continued ill-health compelled him to give up all regular pastoral duties.

At the kind invitation of Sir Thomas and Lady Abney, Watts repaired to their country seat at Theobalds, in Hertfordshire, for a change of air. The visit, intended for a week, resulted in a prolonged stay of thirty years, where he was a loved and honoured guest. At all times, and under varied circumstances, the poet-preacher remembered God, and sought to glorify Him in the furnace of affliction. And God remembered him, "giving him songs in the night, songs in the house of his pilgrimage, songs that make him to the end of time, a tower of strength to the weak and desponding, and indeed a veritable inspiration to all sorts and conditions of men."

Dr. Watts died on November 25th, 1748, at the age of seventy-four, and was buried in the Puritan resting-place at Bunhill Fields, London, not far from the grave of John Bunyan.

Watts wrote about six hundred hymns, and there are few hymnal collections in use to-day which do not contain many of his compositions. Of all his hymns, "When I survey the wondrous cross," is perhaps, the finest. But Watts gave to posterity many others of outstanding merit, chief among which we have:

> O God, our help in ages past,
> Our hope for years to come,
> Our shelter from the stormy blast,
> And our eternal home.

HYMNS AND THEIR WRITERS. 31

This hymn, which in the original is given, "Our God, our help," is a paraphrase of the 90th Psalm, and was first published in 1719. Possibly because of its frequent use on eventful occasions, at times of national stress, as well as at times of public thanksgiving, this grand old hymn has endeared itself to us in a peculiar and fascinating way.

Many of the hymns of Watts were sung for the first time from manuscript by his congregation, the object being that he might accentuate the teaching he had endeavoured to carry to the hearts of his hearers.

Especially is this observed in the following forcible lines, where the writer emphasises the value and virtue of Christ's atoning death:

> Not all the blood of beasts,
> On Jewish altars slain,
> Could give the guilty conscience peace,
> Or wash away one stain.

A story is told of a young Jewess who was saved in a remarkable way through this hymn. She had been out shopping, and had returned home with the provisions for her household. When unwrapping some paper from a package the first verses of this hymn caught her eye, and she read on. This was strange news to her, and try as she would, she was unable to shake off the impression created by such startling words; so she obtained a Bible and eagerly sought the truth. It was thus that the young Jewess found in Jesus the true Messiah and Lord, through whom she obtained eternal redemption.

It was one of Watts' hymns that was used in the conversion of Fanny Crosby, the blind hymn writer. But long before that November day in 1850, and since then, many a seeking soul has been drawn to the foot of the cross at the sweet sound of the same tender lines:

> Alas! and did my Saviour bleed?
> And did my Sovereign die?
> Would He devote that sacred head
> For such a worm as I?

Other hymns by Dr. Watts in frequent use amongst the various assemblies are, "Come, let us join our cheerful songs," "Unto the Lamb that once was slain," "With joy we meditate the grace," and that exultant song of praise so fittingly set to the old Psalm tune "Darwells"—

> Join all the glorious names
> Of wisdom, love and power,
> That mortals ever knew,
> That angels ever bore;
> All are too mean to speak His worth,
> Too mean to set our Saviour forth.

We are indebted to Watts for that fine missionary hymn, "Jesus shall reign," which equals in popularity, even if it does not altogether surpass Reginald Heber's "From Greenland's icy mountains." Throughout the world it has been sung at missionary meetings of almost every Christian denomination; but surely on no more remarkable occasion than when it was sung by a great gathering of native Christians in the South Sea Islands. Their king, having been rescued from the power of sin and darkness, bestowed on his nation a new constitution, exchanging a heathen for a Christian form of government. "Under the spreading branches of the banyan trees," writes Mr. G. J. Stevenson when describing the incident, "sat some thousand natives from Tonga, Fiji and Samoa, on Whit-Sunday, 1862, assembled for divine worship. Foremost amongst them all sat King George himself. Around him were seated

HYMNS AND THEIR WRITERS. 33

old chiefs and warriors who had shared with him the dangers and fortunes of many a battle—men whose eyes were dim, and whose powerful frames were bowed down with the weight of years. But old and young alike rejoiced together in the joys of that day, their faces, most of them radiant with Christian joy, love and hope." It would be impossible to describe the deep feeling manifested when the solemn service began, by the entire audience singing Dr. Watts' hymn:

> Jesus shall reign where e'er the sun
> Does his successive journeys run;
> His kingdom stretch from shore to shore,
> Till moons shall wax and wane no more.

What a memorable day that must have been! Those dark-skinned natives, whose lives had been spent in heathenism of the basest description, were that day met for the first time under a Christian constitution, and with Christ Himself reigning in the hearts of most of them, they doubtless realised in a peculiar way, the truth of the words they sang:

> Blessings abound where e'er He reigns;
> The prisoner leaps to loose his chains;
> The weary find eternal rest,
> And all the sons of want are blest.

AUGUSTUS M. TOPLADY.

> Rock of Ages, cleft for me,
> Let me hide myself in Thee;
> Let the water and the blood,
> From Thy riven side which flowed,
> Be of sin the double cure:
> Save me from its guilt and power.

SO much has been written, and so many stories have, from time to time, been told regarding this famous hymn, that one feels it is hardly necessary to bestow on it more than a passing reference. And yet, familiar though we may be with many remarkable circumstances associated with it, this volume would be incomplete without the inclusion of at least some cursory notes pertaining to this widely known and much loved hymn.

Its author, Augustus Montague Toplady, was born at Farnham, Surrey, in 1740. His father, who was an officer in the British Army, died during the siege of Carthagena soon after the birth of his son.

When Augustus was sixteen years old, he was taken by his mother to Ireland. One evening, when passing a barn in Codymain, the lad was attracted to the humble building by singing which proceeded from it. On entering, he found a few country folks gathered together. When the hymn was ended, a plain uneducated man stood up to preach, taking for his text, "Ye, who sometimes were far off, are made nigh by the blood" (Eph. 2. 13). That sermon was used of God in the salvation of his soul. "By the grace of God, under the ministry of that dear messenger and under that sermon," adds Toplady, "I was, I trust, brought nigh by the blood of Christ, in August, 1756. Strange that I, who had so long sat under the means of grace in England, should be brought near to God in an obscure part of Ireland, amidst a handful of God's people, met together in a barn, and under the ministry of one who could hardly spell his own name."

Toplady wrote many hymns, but few have survived, and it is not at all improbable that his name would have been unknown to-day but for "Rock of Ages." It was written under remarkable circumstances, about three years before his death, which occurred at Hembury, Devonshire, on August 11th, 1778, at the comparatively early age of thirty-eight.

Toplady was curate-in-charge of the parish of Blagdon, on the Mendips, a few miles from Weston-super-Mare. Returning home one day, he was overtaken by a violent thunderstorm, when passing through Burrington Combe, a rocky glen which runs up into the heart of the Mendip Range. There being no habitation near at hand, he took refuge between two massive pillars of rock. It was here, sheltering from the fury of the storm, that Toplady received the inspiration which gave birth to his famous hymn.

On a recent summer afternoon we journeyed along the desolate pass towards the Mendips. At one point of the rugged slopes of grey rock, there is a precipitous crag of limestone, about 100 feet in height, and right down its centre is a deep fissure. Here we halted, that I might obtain the accompanying photograph, and as we peered into the safe retreat of the cleft rock, we found ourselves involuntarily repeating the words which, from generation to generation, have brought comfort and solace to unnumbered hosts:

> Rock of Ages, cleft for me,
> Let me hide myself in Thee!

CHARLES WESLEY.

IT is a remarkable circumstance that at this particular period of national turmoil, when pleasure and recklessness, sin and unbelief, followed each other in quick succession, birth was given to at least two famous hymns which to-day take a prominent place in the very forefront of English hymnody. The hymn which was to become the companion of the one already under review is a composition of equal worth:

> Jesus, Lover of my soul,
>   Let me to Thy bosom fly;
> While the nearer waters roll,
>   While the tempest still is high!
> Hide me, O my Saviour, hide,
>   Till the storm of life is past,
> Safe into the haven guide;
>   O receive my soul at last!

The date of its composition—the year 1739—indicates that this was one of Charles Wesley's first hymns, it having been written soon after his thirtieth birthday. The original has five verses, the third being now omitted. This hymn delineates so faithfully the desires and aspirations of every true believer in the Lord Jesus, that it has become a special favourite among Christians of all denominations.

Though the figure of speech may vary as the hymn proceeds, yet the grand thought of the writer is maintained throughout. Thus in one line is depicted a storm-tossed voyager on the sea of life crying out for shelter until the tempest is past, while in another we can picture the timid, tearful child of God nestling closer and still closer to the tender Lover of souls, as come the faltering words:

> Other refuge have I none;
>   Hangs my helpless soul on Thee!
> Leave, ah, leave me not alone,
>   Still support and comfort me!

HYMNS AND THEIR WRITERS. 37

Many pretty stories still linger around the origin of this hymn. One is that as Wesley sat in his study, a little bird, pursued by a hawk, flew into the open window, and sought refuge in the breast of his coat, where the baffled hawk did not dare to follow. This and other stories, charming and romantic though they may appear, have no foundation of fact, and the most that can be said is that "Jesus, Lover of my soul" was written shortly after the conversion of the author.

Charles Wesley, the youngest of nineteen children, was born at Epworth Rectory, Lincolnshire, in the year 1708. He is credited with having published more than six thousand hymns, and left behind him at his death two thousand in manuscript. In this vast number it is not to be wondered at that, owing, doubtless, to the trend of the times, a large percentage of Wesley's hymns have fallen into disuse; nevertheless, there are a considerable number of outstanding merit which are still amongst our best loved hymns.

His strenuous advocacy of the use of hymns in public worship, in conjunction with his illustrious brother, John, powerfully influenced the course of English hymnody. He died on March 29th, 1788, in his eighty-first year.

Pages might be filled with incidents associated with Charles Wesley's most famous hymn. Years ago, a vessel, while approaching the English coast in a terrific gale, met with disaster, and all on board perished. After the catastrophe, a huge wave carried the shattered wreck up among the rocks, where the ebbing tide left it high and dry. In the captain's cabin a hymn book was found lying on the table. It was opened at a particular page, and in it still lay the pencil which had marked the favourite lines of the Christian sailor.

While the storm raged outside, the captain had drawn a pencil line beneath these words of cheer:

> Jesus, Lover of my soul,
> Let me to Thy bosom fly,
> While the nearer waters roll,
> While the tempest still is high.

WILLIAM COWPER.

> There is a fountain filled with blood,
> Drawn from Immanuel's veins,
> And sinners plunged beneath that flood
> Lose all their guilty stains.

THIS hymn, despite the many arrows levelled at it by the modern critic, has lost none of its old-time power, and is possibly one of the most sung Gospel hymns of the last century.

William Cowper, the author, was born at the Rectory of Berkhampstead, just two hundred years ago. He had a chequered life. Delicate from childhood, he became sensitive and morbid, with frequent fits of melancholy. Trials and afflictions seemed to beset him, more or less, all the days of his life, relieved only by brief seasons of happiness, spent in the company of his friend and compeer, John Newton, at Olney. In his sixth year, Cowper lost his mother, who was the joy of his tender heart. Till the end of his life, the memory of his mother was to him ever green, and years after her death he found fullest expression of his pent-up love in the exquisite poem, "In Memoriam."

Educated at the famous Westminster School, where he had for a class-fellow Warren Hastings, he was afterwards apprenticed to an attorney, and called to the bar. Public life with its constant strain and perpetual bustle, was too much for his nervous temperament, and Cowper was compelled to relinquish his profession. He retired to the home of a friend at Huntingdon, removing later to Olney, where he first met John Newton, the author of "How sweet the name of Jesus sounds." After the two friends had lived together for some time, Newton, with the object of overcoming the ever recurring fits of despondency, suggested that Cowper should assist him in writing what is now known as the "Olney Hymns." Eager to occupy his time in a pursuit well pleasing to his literary tastes, as well as his spiritual aspirations, Cowper at once acted on the suggestion, and many gems of sacred song came from his pen. Probably the best known is:

> God moves in a mysterious way,
> His wonders to perform;
> He plants His footsteps in the sea,
> And rides upon the storm.

The story of how this hymn came to be written has often been told, but is worth recording here. During a fit of mental distress, the poet became possessed with the idea that he should go to a particular part of the River Ouse, and drown himself. The night was dark, and the coachman, purposely losing his way, brought Cowper safely back to his home again. By this time the cloud seemed to have lifted from his mind, and in deep contrition and thankfulness to God for his deliverance from danger and from death, he wrote this hymn, which, for more than a century and a half, has brought comfort and consolation to many a troubled heart.

During these dark and depressing periods, besides the writing of verse, Cowper engaged his attention in various everyday pursuits, such as carpentering, gardening, and the tending of tame hares and other playmates.

The house at Olney in which the poet lived, is now the Cowper Museum. Attached to it is the garden, laid out as it was in the days when William Cowper wandered among the flower-beds, or sat in the shady summer-house, a secluded spot to which the hymn writer would often steal, when the poetic impulse was upon him.

That the hymns of Cowper are not forgotten, even by the present generation, is shown by the fact that in 1931, people from many parts of the country journeyed to Olney, the home of the poet for many years, to witness the celebration of the bi-centenary of his birth, which took place on November 26th, 1731. In the Market Square of this quaint town there gathered a large number of school children, who had assembled to sing some of Cowper's best known hymns, and to listen to an address given on the life story of the poet.

In the parlour of Cowper's house, may be seen the manuscripts of many of his poems, also original letters, the poet's walking-stick, coffee-pot, and numerous mementoes of those far-off days. It was to this room, on that tragic night already referred to, that Cowper retired, and it is not improbable that it was upon the sofa, which may still be seen, the poet wrote his well-known hymn, "God moves in a mysterious way." On entering his bedroom, the visitor cannot but be impressed by the various objects that meet his gaze; and the

COWPER'S PARLOUR
Showing the poet's sofa and other relics. It was in this room that
he wrote the hymn, "God moves in a mysterious way."

THE SUMMER HOUSE.
The birthplace of many of Cowper's hymns.
By kind permission of The Cowper Society.

mind involuntarily wanders over years long past and gone. It was here that the immortal poem, "Toll for the brave," was written. It was his favourite room, and in the quietude of this chamber many of his best hymns were composed, including the sublime lines:

> Oh for a closer walk with God,
> A calm and heavenly frame;
> A light to shine upon the road
> That leads me to the Lamb!

As a sacred poet Cowper takes a prominent place. Of the three hundred and forty-eight "Olney Hymns"—a collection of hymns of outstanding merit, composed at this time by John Newton and William Cowper—sixty-eight were written by the latter, a goodly number of which are to be found in most of the present-day hymnals.

In later years he removed from Olney, and died at East Dereham, on April 25th, 1800.

The hymns of Cowper invariably strike a plaintive note, and lack the element of brightness which characterise the compositions of Watts and Wesley. Of all the hymns from the pen of Cowper, the sweetest and most tender is the universally loved composition:

> Hark, my soul! it is the Lord,
> 'Tis thy Saviour, hear His word;
> Jesus speaks, and speaks to thee,
> "Say, poor sinner, lov'st thou Me?
>
> "I delivered thee when bound,
> And, when bleeding, healed thy wound;
> Sought thee wand'ring, set thee right;
> Turned thy darkness into light."

JOHN NEWTON.

> How sweet the name of Jesus sounds
> In a believer's ear!
> It soothes his sorrows, heals his wounds,
> And drives away his fear.

AT all times, and in practically every circumstance of life, few hymns have charmed the heart of the child of God more than this beautiful composition. And in all probability, had John Newton written no other hymn, this one alone would have made his name famous in the realm of hymnody. Reference has already been made to Newton's association with William Cowper and the "Olney Hymns." To this collection the author of "How sweet the name of Jesus sounds," contributed 280.

Few hymn writers had a more romantic and eventful life than John Newton. He was born in London in 1725. His mother, a godly, consistent Christian, stored his young mind with Scripture truths, but died when her only child was seven years old. At the age of eleven, John was taken to sea by his father, who was a captain in the Merchant Service. After making several voyages, he was one day seized by the Press Gang, and taken on board one of H.M. Warships. Associating with loose and depraved companions, young Newton threw aside the religious restraint of his early training, and became a wicked and abandoned sailor.

Tiring of the rigid discipline of the Royal Navy, he deserted his ship, for which he was publicly flogged at Plymouth, and later was dismissed for insubordination. Soon after, he took service on board a West African slaver, and for a time was engaged in the slave traffic.

HYMNS AND THEIR WRITERS. 43

It was during a terrific storm at sea, when toiling at the pumps in face of apparent death, that the conscience of the godless young sailor was awakened, and he cried aloud to God for mercy. This was the first prayer that had passed his lips for many years. The ship reached port, but the conviction of his sinful condition aroused by the thoughts of that awful night at sea, gave him no peace till he obtained rest for his troubled soul through the merits of the atoning blood of Jesus. Newton abandoned his seafaring life, and received an appointment as tide-surveyor at Liverpool.

He now turned his attention to the study of the Scriptures, and eventually coming under the influence of such men as John Wesley and George Whitefield, Newton became imbued with the desire to preach the Gospel. The greater part of his spare time was given up to preparation for the Lord's work, and after eight years at Liverpool he became curate of Olney, in Buckinghamshire. As already stated, it was here that Newton formed a life-long acquaintance with William Cowper. Most of the hymns of Newton were written at Olney, including the rugged, yet inspiring composition:

> Begone, unbelief! my Saviour is near,
> And for my relief will surely appear;
> By prayer let me wrestle, and He will perform;
> With Christ in the vessel, I smile at the storm.

In 1779, Newton became Rector of St. Mary's Woolnoth, Lombard Street, London, where for twenty-seven years his powerful preaching attracted large crowds, and it is said that no London clergyman of that day exercised a greater influence than did John Newton. His zeal in pastoral visiting and prayer meetings was unwearied. A few years before his death, when pressed by his friends to give up preaching, his reply was characteristic of the man: "What," said he, "shall the old African blasphemer stop while he can speak?" And when, with increasing age, his memory was almost completely gone, Newton would remark to those who sought to comfort him: "Though my memory is failing, I can never forget two things; first, that I was a great sinner, and second, that Jesus is a great Saviour." Truly, he realised in his soul that he owed everything to Jesus, the sound of whose name had touched the tender chords of his heart, and in the effulgence of joy came the words:

> Dear Name! the rock on which I build!
> My shield and hiding-place!
> My never failing treasury, filled
> With boundless stores of grace.

Newton was a man of fervent prayer, thus it is not surprising that many of his compositions strike the tender note of supplication. Amongst these there is one of surpassing beauty, which is still a favourite at our prayer meetings:

> Behold the throne of grace!
> The promise calls us near,
> To seek our God and Father's face,
> Who loves to answer prayer.
>
> Beyond our utmost wants
> His love and power can bless;
> To praying souls he always grants
> More than they can express.

When Newton was nearly fourscore years, he was almost blind, and could with great difficulty read his manuscript sermon, so a friend stood behind him in the pulpit to assist the aged preacher during the service. One Lord's Day, while proceeding with his address, Newton had twice read the words, "Jesus Christ is precious." "You have already said that twice," whispered his helper; "go on, sir." "John," was Newton's quick reply, "I

HYMNS AND THEIR WRITERS.

said that twice, and I am going to say it again." And raising his voice again, he cried with renewed emphasis, "Jesus is precious!" John Newton died on December 21st, 1807, at the advanced age of eighty-two.

Besides these already quoted, other hymns by Newton to be found in our hymnals are, "Great Shepherd of Thy chosen flock," "Let us love, and sing, and wonder!" "Let us rejoice in Christ our Lord," "Poor, weak, and worthless though I am," "Sweeter sounds than music knows," and the short yet expressive parting hymn so often used as a doxology:

> May the grace of Christ our Saviour,
>   And the Father's boundless love,
> With the Holy Spirit's favour,
>   Rest upon us from above!
>
> Thus may we abide in union,
>   With each other and the Lord,
> And possess in sweet communion,
>   Joys which earth can ne'er afford.

PHILIP DODDRIDGE.

> Grace! 'tis a charming sound,
> Harmonious to the ear;
> Heaven with the echo shall resound,
> And all the earth shall hear.

PHILIP DODDRIDGE, the author of this inspiring hymn, was born in London, on June 26th, 1702. He was the twentieth child of his parents, and had the priceless heritage of a godly mother. Writing of his early days, Doddridge tells us that before he could read, his mother taught him the Scriptures by the assistance of some blue Dutch tiles; and that these Bible stories, so crudely illustrated in this unique fashion, were the means of creating an impression upon his young heart, which had a lasting effect. There may, to-day, be seen in Holyrood Palace, Edinburgh, similar tiles built into one of the fire-places in the historic building. Remembering this incident in the childhood of Philip Doddridge, I was greatly interested when our guide informed us of the very practical use to which these tiles, bearing pictures of Bible subjects, had been put, when the family gathered round a blazing log fire, during the long winter evenings, in those far-off days, when few were able to read, and books were only in the possession of the well-to-do.

At the age of ten Philip was sent to the Grammar School at Kingston-upon-Thames, but his father dying three years later, the boy was removed to another school. It was about this time that the religious training received in his early life began to manifest itself in a very marked way, and we find his spare time almost wholly taken up in visiting poor cottagers in the district, to

HYMNS AND THEIR WRITERS.   47

whom he read the Scriptures, thus giving early promise of his future usefulness.

When quite a youth, Philip Doddridge began preaching the Gospel, and before he had reached the age of twenty-one, he was appointed minister of the Congregational Church at Kibworth. After seven years pastorate, he removed to Northampton, where the remainder of a strenuous life, ungrudgingly spent in the service of the Lord, was hastened to a close by consumption. In the hope of arresting the malady, Dr. Doddridge was ordered to leave England, and he sailed for Lisbon, where he died on October 26th, 1751, within a fortnight of his arrival, in his 50th year.

Though Dr. Doddridge is best remembered as a hymn writer, he was known in his day as a writer of marked literary ability. His best prose work, "The Rise and Progress of Religion in the Soul," was long cherished in evangelical circles because of its great spiritual worth. In the production of this and other literary works, he received much encouragement and assistance from his aged friend and fellow hymn writer, Isaac Watts.

It is a remarkable circumstance that the hymns of Doddridge, which were widely circulated in manuscript form, and had already gained no small measure of popularity in his life time, were not published till after his death. Many of the original copies in the author's own clear handwriting, though now worn and faded, are still preserved.

Dr. Doddridge wrote about 400 hymns. Of that number there is one, which, in the days of our first love, was ever on our lips, and though many summers have passed since the glad day of our new birth, yet, to many of us this hymn has lost none of its charm and sweetness:

> O happy day, that fixed my choice
> On Thee, my Saviour and my God!
> Well may this glowing heart rejoice,
> And tell its raptures all abroad.

But the one hymn by Doddridge, around which, since the day it was written, nearly 200 years ago, has gathered so many tender and touching associations, is that whose opening stanzas are:

> O God of Bethel, by whose hand
> Thy people still are fed,
> Who through this weary pilgrimage
> Hast all our fathers led.
>
> Our vows, our prayers we now present
> Before Thy throne of grace;
> God of our Fathers, be the God
> Of their succeeding race.

The original manuscript of this hymn is a treasured possession of the descendants of Colonel Gardiner, a devoted Christian and friend of Doddridge, who was killed at the battle of Preston Pans, during the 'Forty-five Rebellion. It formerly belonged to Lady Frances Erskine, an intimate acquaintance of the author.

WILLIAM WILLIAMS.

WHILE Philip Doddridge was ministering to the needs of his devoted flock at Northampton, utilising his leisure moments in the writing of hymns, which were to be a solace and consolation to generations yet unborn, a Welshman, imbued with the religious fire and fervour of his native land, was storing away in his note-book the poetical outpourings of a heart attuned to God. His name was William Williams, and from his little collection of songs, which were first inscribed to be sung in his native tongue, one composition at once caught the ear of the singing public, and has since been carried on the wings of song from continent to continent. It is a hymn of the Christian pilgrim praying for guidance, and opens with the verse:

> Guide me, O Thou great Jehovah!
> Pilgrim through this barren land;
> I am weak but Thou art mighty;
> Hold me with Thy powerful hand.
> Bread of heaven! Bread of heaven!
> Feed me now and evermore!

To enter into the true spirit of this hymn, is to hear it sung in parts to the typically Welsh tune "Cwm Rhondda."

Williams was born at Cefn-y-Coed, near Llandovery, in 1717, and was intended for the medical profession, but, coming under the vigorous preaching of Howell Harris, he was converted, after which he turned his attention to the ministry. When he was yet in his early twenties, Williams became a curate of the Church of England, but as he associated himself with George Whitefield, going about from parish to parish preaching the Gospel, he was summoned before the Bishop from time to time. Instead of damping his zeal, the fire kindled in the bosom of the young Welshman, seemed to burst forth, with the result that he threw aside all ecclesiastical restraint, and for forty-five years went everywhere preaching the Word. William Williams died at Pantycelyn on January 11th, 1791.

Of the sweet singer of Wales, Dr. David Walker has ably written: "While the vocation of this worthy Welsh personality was undoubtedly to preach the glorious Gospel of the blessed God, and to tell with trumpet tongue of that love divine that is so old in origin, so free in outflow, so eternal in duration, so universal in embrace, so boundless in blessings, he crowned it all with the gift of song, and for his many melodies he merits the epithet of the sweet singer of his native land, the Watts of Wales." It is said that in carrying the "Good News" from village to village, over hill and moor and glen, Williams travelled every year, summer and winter, over two thousand miles during the forty-five years of his labour in the service of the Lord.

As a poet, Williams merited and received the praise of his contemporaries. During his lifetime he published one or two collections of hymns which ran into several editions, his most widely known composition being the hymn already quoted.

JAMES MONTGOMERY.

> Prayer is the soul's sincere desire,
>   Uttered or unexpressed,
> The motion of a hidden fire
>   That trembles in the breast.
>
> Prayer is the Christian's vital breath,
>   The Christian's native air;
> His watchword at the gates of death;
>   He enters heaven with prayer.

WHEN James Montgomery laid down his pen after composing these sublime lines, which so lucidly define, in true poetic language, the mystic meaning of prayer—understood by experience, yet ofttimes difficult to express in words—he bequeathed a hymn of supplication, which, to the child of God, becomes dearer with the passing of years.

The son of a Moravian minister of Irish descent, James Montgomery was born on November 4th, 1771, at Irvine, in Ayrshire, the land made famous as the native place of Robert Burns. His father was anxious that James, his eldest son, should follow in his footsteps, and sent the boy to a Moravian school at Fulneck, in Yorkshire, to pursue his studies. Not long afterwards, the parents, responding to a call to the Lord's work in the foreign field, sailed as missionaries to the West Indies, where, after a brief service, they died, leaving their son to fight life's battle single-handed.

Left to his own resources, it was not long before young Montgomery, tiring of the restraint of school life, and feeling his utter unfitness for ministerial duties, abandoned all thought of fulfilling the purpose of his father. Escaping from school he set out in search of work, and obtained employment at a retail shop at Mirfield, near Wakefield. This change, however, did not exactly suit his youthful taste, and for a time afterwards he seemed to be like the proverbial stone that gathers no moss. His next employment was in the shop of a draper at Wath-upon-Dearne. All this time the youthful poet was busy writing verses, and before he had reached his eighteenth birthday he had collected quite a considerable number of poems. Fired with ambition he made a journey to London—quite a big undertaking in those days—with the hope of finding a publisher for his poems. To his great disappointment this ended in failure, and he returned to Sheffield, where he secured an appointment in the office of the "Sheffield Register" newspaper. Montgomery eventually became proprietor, changed its name to "Iris," and successfully conducted it for thirty years.

As a journalist, his principles in days when party feeling ran high, were evidently too liberal for the Government's ideas, and Montgomery was twice imprisoned, once for publishing a poem—not his own—on the Fall of the Bastille. It was when Montgomery lay in prison that many of his best hymns were written. In after years, perhaps by way of atonement for their misdeeds, the Government conferred on the poet a well-deserved pension of £200 a year.

Recognized as a poet of high water mark, Montgomery's compositions brought him considerable popularity, and called forth the admiration of such critics as the celebrated Lord Byron.

James Montgomery was once asked—"Which of your poems will live?" to which he replied, "None, sir, except a few of my hymns." He spoke truly. It is by his hymns that Montgomery

HYMNS AND THEIR WRITERS.

is remembered, rather than by his more ambitious poetry. Thus, while many of his classical poems which brought him fame as a poet are unknown to-day, such hymns as the following composition, which has brought consolation to many a troubled heart in the hour of trial, will never be forgotten:

> For ever with the Lord!
>   Amen, so let it be:
> Life from the dead is in that word,
>   'Tis immortality.
> Here in the body pent,
>   Absent from Him I roam;
> Yet nightly pitch my moving tent
>   A day's march nearer home.

As a writer of sacred song James Montgomery has made quite a reputation, and of the four hundred hymns he wrote, a considerable number are in popular use to-day. Special mention should be made of that sweetest of all communion hymns, reminiscent of hallowed moments spent around the Lord's Table:

> According to Thy gracious Word,
>   In meek humility,
> This will I do, my dying Lord,
>   I will remember Thee.

Dr. Julian, the eminent hymnologist, has this to say of Montgomery: "The secrets of his power as a writer of hymns were manifold. His poetic genius was of a high order, higher than most who stood with him in the front rank of Christian poets. His knowledge of the Holy Scriptures was most extensive. His religious views were broad and charitable. His devotional spirit was of the holiest type. With the faith of a strong man he united the beauty and simplicity of a child."

James Montgomery died at Sheffield on April 30th, 1854, at the advanced age of eighty-three, and was accorded a public funeral.

A verse from one of his best loved hymns, beautifully expresses the glorious anticipation the poet cherished of heaven and its everlasting glories:

>My Father's house on high,
> Home of my soul, how near
>At times, to faith's foreseeing eye,
> The golden gates appear!
>
>Ah! then my spirit faints
> To reach the land I love,
>The bright inheritance of saints,
> Jerusalem above.

JOHN BAKEWELL.

> Hail, Thou once despiséd Jesus!
> Hail, Thou still rejected King!
> Thou didst suffer to release us,
> Thou didst free salvation bring;
> Through Thy death and resurrection,
> Bearer of our sin and shame!
> We enjoy divine protection,
> Life and glory through Thy name.

AWAY back, nearly two hundred years, when Augustus Toplady was writing his immortal hymn "Rock of Ages," and Charles Wesley, having given to the world "Jesus Lover of my soul," was busy with his pen, filling notebook after notebook with hymns, to the number of many thousands, there lived two men, intimate friends of their more illustrious contemporaries, who each committed to paper, a hymn which was willed of God to be sung for many generations to come. They were close friends, and though in their day they wrote not a few hymns, yet, as in the case of many other writers, their names are remembered by a single composition each.

The name of one was John Bakewell. He was born at Brailsford, Derbyshire, and lived to the great age of ninety-eight. His tombstone in City Road Chapel burial ground, near by the tomb of John Wesley, bears this splendid testimony: "He adorned the doctrine of God our Saviour eighty years, and preached His glorious Gospel about seventy years." His hymn "Hail, Thou once despised Jesus!" was given by the author to Toplady, who, after making a few slight alterations, published it with several of his own compositions. Since then, its jubilant note of praise has not ceased to ascend to Him the source of all our joy.

THOMAS OLIVERS.

IT is said that while Bakewell lived at Westminster, where he was well-known as a Wesleyan local preacher, his friend Thomas Olivers called, and while the two were together, Olivers wrote his majestic hymn:

> The God of Abraham praise,
> Who reigns enthroned above,
> Ancient of everlasting days,
> And God of love.
> Jehovah, great I AM!
> By earth and heaven confessed,
> I bow and bless the sacred name,
> For ever blessed.

Thomas Olivers was born at Tregynon, Montgomeryshire, in 1725. At the age of four he lost both parents, and was brought up by a distant relative, who, when the boy was old enough, had him apprenticed to a shoemaker. His youth was marked by fits of wanton wickedness, and in order to escape public indignation through his misconduct, he was obliged to leave the neighbourhood.

Journeying from place to place, the young profligate eventually reached Bristol in a state of abject poverty and wretchedness. One day, while wandering about the streets in search of food and shelter, he chanced to hear George Whitefield, the celebrated evangelist, preach from the text "Is not this a brand plucked out of the fire?" (Zech. 3. 2). That sermon was the means of Olivers' conversion, and he became a decided Christian. Securing employment at Bradford-on-Avon, he worked at his trade of shoemaking till he was able to pay off all the debts he had incurred in his unregenerate days, and at once took to preaching the Gospel. It was here that he met John Wesley, who, recognizing both the ability and zeal of Olivers, persuaded him to give up his present occupation and become one of his preachers.

He at once proceeded as an evangelist to Cornwall, and continued a faithful minister of the Gospel till his death nearly fifty years later, having visited most of the large towns in England, as well as journeying as far north as Aberdeen.

It is, of course, as the author of "The God of Abraham praise," that the name of Thomas Olivers is perpetuated; a hymn of which so distinguished a writer as James Montgomery declares, "There is not in our language a lyric of more majestic style."

Regarding the origin of the hymn, it is said that Olivers received the inspiration on hearing a certain Dr. Leoni sing an old Hebrew melody. He wrote the stirring words to the tune to which it is still sung, and which to-day is known by "Leoni."

A difficult measure, the hymn has been composed with remarkable skill, an outstanding feature being the frequent Scriptural allusions, so gracefully portrayed and expressed:

> The God of heaven praise,
>   At Whose supreme command
> From earth I rise, and seek my joys
>   At His right hand.
> He calls me to forsake
>   Earth's wisdom, fame and power,
> And Him my only portion make,
>   My shield and tower.

The mention of this hymn recalls the faithful labours of the late Mr. Alpheus Wilkes, who visited the various assemblies throughout the country nearly two decades ago, ministering the

Word to believers. Formerly a clergyman in the Church of England, Mr. Wilkes still retained the austere bearing of his ecclesiastical training. Especially was this the case in the choice of his hymns. With Mr. Wilkes there was only one hymn, and it was no unusual occurrence to hear "The God of Abraham praise" announced from the platform at almost every service, despite the fact that the singing of the difficult and rather tantalising melody was not always rendered in a fashion likely to please even the least sensitive musical ear.

A touching incident is related in connection with this hymn. A young Jewess had recently put her trust in the Saviour, and her subsequent baptism so enraged her father, who was the chief of his synagogue, that he threatened to kill his daughter.

The girl found refuge in the house of the one who had pointed her to the Saviour; "and there," says an eye-witness, who was afterwards brought to Christ by the scene, "I saw her, in the hour of bitterness, when the reality of her abandonment by the house of her fathers first came upon her. It did not damp her joy in Christ Jesus, and I shall never forget the scene when she stood, with clasped hands, her black lustrous eyes upturned to heaven, and her dark but expressive face lighted up, and lifting up her voice sang snatches of what she had already learned to call her own hymn."

> The God of Abraham praise,
>   Whose all-sufficient grace
> Shall guide me all my pilgrim days,
>   In all my ways;
> He calls a worm His friend,
>   He calls Himself my God,
> And He shall save me to the end,
>   Through Jesus' blood.

ROBERT MURRAY McCHEYNE.

I once was a stranger to grace and to God,
I knew not my danger and felt not my load:
Though friends spoke in rapture of Christ on the tree,
JEHOVAH TSIDKENU was nothing to me.

My terrors all vanished before the sweet name;
My guilty fears banished, with boldness I came
To drink at the fountain, life-giving and free:
JEHOVAH TSIDKENU is all things to me.

AFTER the passing of well nigh a century, "Jehovah Tsidkenu" (The Lord my Righteousness) has lost none of its old-time charm. To-day, as then, its sweet yet rugged simplicity marks it down as a hymn beloved. Claiming no high literary merit, but aiming only to voice the deep, unfathomable joys of a soul redeemed by the precious blood of Christ, this old-fashioned testimony hymn has sung its way into the hearts of ransomed ones, from the first days of the Victorian era until the present time.

Robert Murray McCheyne was but a youth of twenty-one when, one bleak November day in 1834, just as he was recovering from an attack of fever, which had laid him aside on a sick-bed, he wrote the hymn, inseparably associated with a name revered not only in the land of his birth, but wherever these spiritual heart-breathings of a first love have found an honoured place.

He was born in Edinburgh on May 21st, 1813, and was the youngest child of the family. At school he made rapid progress, and at an early period became somewhat eminent among his fellows. At that time there were held in the Tron Church, in the interval between sermons, what our good Scottish forefathers reverently regarded as catechetical exercise. Accompanied by his parents, Robert was regular in his attendance on such occasions, and it was then that interest was aroused in the boy's sweet recitation of the Psalms and passages of Scripture.

After a period of six years, spent at the High School, where he gained some distinction in literature, he entered the Edinburgh University. Referring to McCheyne at this particular time, Dr. Andrew Bonar, his devoted friend and companion writes: "He had a very considerable knowledge of music, and himself sang correctly and beautifully. This was a gift which was used to the glory of the Lord in after days—wonderfully enlivening his secret devotions, and enabling him to lead the song of praise in the congregation wherever occasion required."

The death of his eldest brother, David, a faithful and promising young Christian, to whom he was greatly attached, was an event which awoke him to realise his condition as a lost sinner. Thus in His wonderful providence, the Lord called one soul to enjoy the boundless riches of His grace, while He took the other into the possession of eternal glory.

It was a few months before leaving college, that Mr. McCheyne wrote "Jehovah Tsidkenu," which reveals the sure and steadfast confidence of his soul. Some days later, on his recovery from the illness which had laid him aside, he wrote in his diary a short poem, commencing:

> He tenderly binds up the broken in heart,
>   The soul bowed down He will raise:
> For mourning, the ointment of joy will impart:
>   For heaviness garments of praise.
>
> Ah, come, then, and sing to the praise of our God,
>   Who giveth and taketh away;
> Who first by His kindness and then by His rod,
>   Would teach us, poor sinners, to pray.

HYMNS AND THEIR WRITERS.

Though still undergoing a student's usual examination before the Presbytery, we find him, at twenty-two, preaching in Annan Church, Dumfriesshire; thus began Robert Murray McCheyne's labours in the Lord's vineyard.

From the early days of his ministry Mr. McCheyne depreciated the custom of reading sermons, believing that to do so greatly weakened the power and freedom of the preacher in delivering his message. Though he possessed the gift of extemporaneous composition, this distinctive endowment did not in the least degree restrain him from making diligent preparation at all times. "The heads of his sermon," said one who was accustomed to hear him preach, "were not the milestones that tell you how near you are to your journey's end, but they were nails which fixed and fastened all he said."

In the year 1836, when he was twenty-three, Mr. McCheyne became minister of Dundee, where during the remaining years of a brief but beautiful life, he laboured with untiring zeal and fervour, the fragrant memory of which is undiminished, even to this day. One of his first efforts was to begin a weekly prayer meeting, and never had he any cause to regret having set apart one night in the week for this purpose, for some of the most precious seasons were at these meetings. Nor did the young minister confine his energies to the older members of his flock, but sought to encourage the various Sunday Schools in his parish. It was in connection with his work among the young, that, in 1841, he wrote the hymn "Oil for the Lamp," in order to impress the parable on a Sunday School class. It is an almost forgotten hymn of sixteen verses, telling in simple language the story of the Ten Virgins, and opens with the stanza:

> Ten virgins clothed in white,
> The Bridegroom went to meet;
> Their lamps were burning bright
> To guide His welcome feet.

Towards the end of his second year's ministry at Dundee, Mr. McCheyne's health broke down—the result of unremitting labour—and his medical adviser insisted on a complete change. This led him to accept an invitation to accompany a party about to set out on a mission to Israel. Murray McCheyne's visit to Palestine, his unbounded joy at being used in carrying salvation to the Jew as he had hitherto done to the Gentile, forms one long interesting record of that memorable mission, and is contained in a diary of these events, which he has left behind.

After an absence of some months, Mr. McCheyne returned to his beloved flock at Dundee, where he was received with the greatest joy. The years following were times of blessing and revival, which spread to many parts of Scotland.

Though Mr. McCheyne wrote a few hymns, one or two of which still survive, his name is best remembered as a faithful and beloved minister of the Gospel, rather than as a hymn writer.

After a comparatively brief ministry of seven years, Robert Murray McCheyne passed into the presence of the Lord, on March 25th, 1843, at the early age of twenty-nine.

Possibly his best loved hymn is the one originally entitled "I am a Debtor." It was written in 1837, and contains nine verses. Few hymn books give more than four verses, these having been selected as the most suitable for public worship. The opening stanza strikes the key note to the theme so tenderly expressed and sustained throughout the hymn:

> When this passing world is done,
> When has sunk yon glaring sun,
> When I stand with Christ on high,
> Looking o'er life's history:
> Then, Lord, shall I fully know—
> Not till then—how much I owe.

JOSEPH HART.

> How good is the God we adore,
>   Our faithful, unchangeable Friend,
> Whose love is as great as His power,
>   And knows neither measure nor end.

THE hymnist, who, in the ecstasy of a heart over-flowing with praise and adoration, penned these lines, was Joseph Hart. He was born in London, in the year 1712. From his parents, who were consistent, God-fearing people, the boy received a good start in life; but, while on occasions he had many serious thoughts at the time of his early manhood, these were stifled by the extravagant indulgences of a careless and wayward life. At last, after years of deep conviction of sin and remorse, followed by periods of gross sin and free-thinking, Hart was soundly converted while listening to a sermon preached from Romans 3. 10, at the Moravian Chapel, Fetters Lane, London. He was then about forty-five. Two years later, he began, in real earnest, both to preach and to write hymns.

That Joseph Hart believed in the truths of the Gospel with a deep personal sincerity is revealed in the preface to one of his hymn books. Here he speaks of his conversion in language which shows how profoundly he had been brought under a sense of sin. Thus he writes: "The Lord, by His spirit of love, came, not in a visionary manner into my brain, but with such divine power and energy into my soul, that I was lost in blissful amazement. I cried out, 'What! me Lord?' His spirit answered, 'Yes, thee! I pardon thee freely and fully!' The alteration I then felt in my soul was as sudden and palpable as that which is experienced by a person staggering and almost sinking under a burden, when it is immediately taken from his shoulders. Jesus Christ and Him crucified is now the only thing I desire to know.

Joseph Hart died on May 24th, 1768, aged fifty-six, and was buried at Bunhill Fields. It is said that his funeral was attended by about twenty thousand people.

The hymns of Hart—many of them of considerable merit—were at one time more widely used than they are to-day. Possibly the best known are: "How good is the God we adore," (which was originally written "This God is the God we adore"). "Come, Holy Spirit, come, and that widely used Gospel hymn:

> Come, ye sinners, poor and wretched,
>   Weak and wounded, sick and sore;
> Jesus ready stands to save you,
>   Full of pity, love, and power:
>   He is able;
>   He is willing: doubt no more.

ROBERT HAWKER.

ANOTHER familiar hymn with which the name of Joseph Hart is associated is, "Once more before we part." This hymn originally appeared in two stanzas, written by Hart about the year 1762. Twenty-five years later, Dr. Robert Hawker, of Plymouth, using the theme of Hart's dismissal hymn, not only altered the original lines, but added three verses and a chorus. "The Believers Hymn Book" in common with others has omitted two verses, and slightly altered the first verse, the original of which reads:

> Once more before we part,
> Bless the Redeemer's name;
> Write it on every heart,
> Speak every tongue the same.

Robert Hawker was born at Exeter, in 1753, and was educated to be a surgeon. He soon afterwards turned his attention to the ministry and became curate of the Church of Charles the Martyr, at Plymouth, where he continued to officiate till his death, which occurred in his seventy-fourth year.

Besides being the author of a few hymns, Dr. Hawker was, in his day, renowned as a distinguished commentator of the Scriptures. Dr. Hawker is the author of a hymn, still in use, beginning with the line, "Lord, dismiss us with Thy blessing." This should not be confused with the better known hymn by Dr. Fawcett, which commences with the same line.

S. Baring Gould, who wrote "Onward, Christian Soldiers," tells a rather amusing story relating to the good doctor. "In Charles' Church," he says, "the evening service always closed with the singing of the hymn, 'Lord, dismiss us with Thy blessing,' composed by Dr. Hawker himself. His grandson did not know the authorship of the hymn; he came to the doctor one day with a paper in his hand, and said, 'Grandfather, I don't altogether like that hymn "Lord, dismiss us with Thy blessing"; I think it might be improved in metre and language, and would be better if made somewhat longer.'

'Oh, indeed!' said Dr. Hawker, getting red; 'and pray, Robert, what amendations commend themselves to your precocious wisdom?'

'This is my improved version,' said the boy, and read:

> 'Lord, dismiss us with Thy blessing,
> High and low, and rich and poor;
> May we all Thy fear possessing,
> Go in peace and sin no more!'—

—and so on to the end of his 'new' version." Then Mr. Baring Gould tells us that the audacious youngster, picking up a hymn book, actually recited to his grandfather the original hymn, and added to his offences by the remark: "This one is crude and flat; don't you think so, grandfather?"

"Crude and flat, sir! Young puppy, it is mine! I wrote that hymn."

"Oh, I beg your pardon, grandfather, I did not know that; it is a very nice hymn indeed; but —but—" and as he went out of the door—"mine is better."

JOHN FAWCETT.

DR. John Fawcett, the hymn writer already referred to, was converted at the age of sixteen, under the ministry of George Whitefield, the noted evangelist. In 1765 he became Baptist minister at Wainsgate, near Hebden Bridge, Yorkshire. Invited to London in 1772 to succeed the celebrated Dr. J. Gill, as pastor of Carter's Lane, he preached his farewell sermon, and a few days later prepared to leave. The wagons, loaded with his household goods, were at the door, when his sorrowing people, many of them in tears, crowded round the good man and his wife, pleading with them not to go. Overcome at such evidence of affection, the faithful pastor decided to give up the idea of the big church in London, and remain with his small but attached flock. It was this incident that suggested the hymn, "Blest be the tie that binds," which he afterwards wrote.

Dr. Fawcett's dismissal hymn, which attained a much greater degree of popularity than Dr. Hawker's, has still a very extensive use. Practically every hymn book of an Evangelical type during the past hundred years, has adopted it in a form more or less perfect. The opening verse has a sweet familiarity:

> Lord, dismiss us with Thy blessing,
>   Fill our hearts with joy and peace;
> Let us each Thy love possessing,
>   Triumph in redeeming grace,
>   Oh! refresh us,
> Travelling through this wilderness.

WALTER SHIRLEY.

> Sweet the moments rich in blessing,
> Which before the Cross we spend,
> Life, and health, and peace possessing
> From the sinner's dying Friend."

THIS hymn, attributed to Walter Shirley, is really a transcript from James Allen's "When my Jesus I'm possessing." Shirley left so little of the original that the hymn is now properly credited to him, instead of to Allen. The Hon. Walter Shirley was the grandson of the first Earl Ferres, and cousin to the Countess of Huntingdon, a name so closely associated with a remarkable period of spiritual revival in England nearly two centuries ago.

Born in 1725, Shirley received an education fitted to his station in life, but, following the dictates of his conscience, after experiencing a great spiritual change, he entered the ministry of the Church of England, and was for some time Rector of Loughrea, County Galway, Ireland. A faithful minister of the Word, his labours brought him in close touch with Whitefield and the Wesleys, in whose chapels he was often to be found preaching the Gospel. In 1774, he revised Lady Huntingdon's celebrated hymn book, a collection used not only in her own chapels, but in other places of worship as well.

Walter Shirley wrote a number of hymns, but very few have survived, and it is not improbable that, but for "Sweet the moments rich in blessing," his name as a hymn writer might have been forgotten. He died in Dublin, April 7th, 1786.

JOHN CENNICK.

THIS period was fairly prolific in producing hymns, many of which are still sung with no less fervour than when they were first penned. This may truly be written of the hymn beginning:

> Brethren let us join to bless
> Jesus Christ, our joy and peace;
> Him, who bowed His head so low
> Underneath our load of woe.

The writer is John Cennick. He was born at Reading, Berkshire, in 1718. Descended from a family of Quakers, the boy had a strict religious upbringing until his thirteenth year. His removal to London at this time, with the object of learning the profession of land surveyor, had injurious effects upon his early training, and he became a wild and reckless youth. Following a period of wanton wickedness, he came under deep conviction of sin while walking along Cheapside, which, after weeks of spiritual anxiety, resulted in his conversion.

Coming under the influence of John Wesley, Cennick was for a time associated with him in his work, both as a preacher of the Gospel and as a teacher of a Wesleyan school for colliers' children at Kingswood. He afterwards assisted George Whitefield, but in 1745, because of doctrinal differences, he joined the Moravians, with whom he became actively associated.

Much of the remainder of his life was spent in the north of Ireland, but he returned to London in a feeble condition of health, and died there, on July 4th, 1755.

Cennick's earlier hymns were written for the use of the Wesleys—who freely amended them, as Charles Wesley admits—and many are still widely used, including his well-known grace before meat, beginning:

> Be present at our table, Lord,
> Be here and everywhere adored.

JOHN MASON.

IN the days of John Bunyan, when the Bedford tinker was busy writing his immortal "Pilgrim's Progress"; when Bishop Ken had given to the world the universally loved doxology, "Praise God from whom all blessings flow"; and when Tate and Brady were composing and compiling their own peculiar type of hymns and psalms, another writer, perhaps less known, in the ecstasy of a new found joy, wrote the hymn:

> I've found the precious Christ of God,
> My heart doth sing for joy;
> And sing I must, for Christ I have,
> A precious Christ have I.

This hymn has been greatly altered from the original, the first verse of which commenced with the line, "I've found the pearl of greatest price." The name of the writer is John Mason. He was the son of a nonconformist minister, but of his early life very little is known. In 1660 he entered Cambridge, where he graduated four years later. About the year 1674 we find him appointed Rector of Water-Stratford, "where the Lord gave him satisfaction in time of famine, and rest in the midst of troublous times round about, for twenty years." He died there in 1694.

Mason was a writer of considerable ability,

though at that period hymns were written for private edification, rather than for public use. It is supposed, however, that he made use of his hymns in public worship, and if so, they are among the earliest hymns so used. A number of his compositions are to be found in the early Hymn Collections of the eighteenth century, and are marked by the purity of spiritual expression. His productions, both prose and poetical, were much eulogised by Isaac Watts, and there is no doubt that the hymns of Mason greatly influenced the compositions both of Watts and Wesley in their day.

Mason was a man of true piety and spirituality, constant in prayer, and effectual in proclaiming the truth of the Scriptures. His close friendship with the saintly Richard Baxter, indicated where his sympathies lay. His favourite theme was the second coming of our Lord, the truth of which was greatly accentuated in his thoughts during the closing days of his life. One night, not many weeks before his death, he is said to have had a remarkable vision of the Lord Jesus. So real did it appear to him, and so deeply was the vision impressed on his mind, that he preached a sermon called "The Midnight Cry," in which he proclaimed the near approach of Christ's Second Advent. The sermon created quite a sensation, and a report quickly spread that the Advent would take place at Water-Stratford itself. Crowds gathered from the neighbouring villages, bringing provisions with them, till almost every corner of the village was occupied. Extraordinary scenes occurred, accompanied by loud and unrestrained singing of the crowd; and the excitement had scarcely died out when the old man passed away, still testifying that he had seen the Lord, and that it was time for the nations to tremble, and for Christians to trim their lamps.

"The frame of his spirit was so heavenly,' says Richard Baxter, "his deportment so humble and obliging, his discourse of spiritual things so weighty, with such apt words and delightful air, that it charmed all that had any spiritual relish.'

John Mason's compositions are contained in "Spiritual Songs," published in 1686, a copy of which—one of the earliest collections of hymns— may be seen in the British Museum.

JOSEPH SCRIVEN.

> What a Friend we have in Jesus,
> All our sins and griefs to bear!
> What a privilege to carry
> Everything to God in prayer!

BUT for a tragic circumstance in the life of a young man, the realm of hymnody might have been poorer to-day, by the absence of this beautiful hymn which has been a solace to many a weary and troubled soul, ever since the day, over half-a-century ago, when "What a Friend we have in Jesus" was written.

Joseph Scriven, the author, was born at Seapatrick, Banbridge, Co. Down, in the year 1820, and graduated at Trinity College, Dublin. He emigrated to Canada when he was twenty-five, and lived a useful life there, until his death at Port Hope, on Lake Ontario, in 1886.

Early in life he sustained a severe loss which

THE GRAVE OF JOSEPH SCRIVEN.
He wrote "What a Friend we have in Jesus."

ROCK OF AGES.
Photo: D. J. Beattie. Where Toplady wrote his famous hymn.

HYMNS AND THEIR WRITERS.

was the means of changing his future career. The young woman to whom he was to be married, was accidentally drowned on the eve of their wedding day. This sad event led Mr. Scriven to consecrate his life and fortune to the service of the Lord, not the least service being the composition of one short hymn; though indeed, the author himself was probably less conscious than anyone else on that particular occasion, that any real or lasting work had been done for the Master.

Though a man of education and refinement, he chose to labour amongst the poor of his neighbourhood, where the greater part of his life was spent, ministering to their spiritual as well as their temporal needs. Of a quiet and unassuming nature, he was beloved by all with whom he came in contact; nor was it an unusual circumstance that found the good man cutting up firewood, and carrying out other such humble duties for the poor and afflicted of his self-appointed charge.

It is not known whether Mr. Scriven wrote another hymn besides "What a Friend we have in Jesus." Indeed, it was not learned that he possessed any poetic gift till shortly before he was called home, when a neighbour, sitting up with him during his last illness, found the manuscript of the hymn amongst some papers. Perusing it with evident delight, he read it over to his sick friend, at the same time questioning him about it. Reluctant to make the admission, Mr. Scriven said he had composed the verses for his mother, to comfort her in a time of special sorrow, not intending that anyone else should see it. Some time later, another Port Hope neighbour on asking Mr. Scriven if it was true that he was the author of the hymn, his reply was: "The Lord and I did it between us."

The second verse, written in the form of question and answer, and couched in simple yet forceful language, breathes encouragement and comfort throughout:

> Have we trials and temptations?
> Is there trouble anywhere?
> We should never be discouraged:
> Take it to the Lord in prayer!
> Can we find a friend so faithful,
> Who will all our sorrows share?
> Jesus knows our every weakness:
> Take it to the Lord in prayer!

Although the hymn had already appeared in a small collection, it was not until 1875, when it came into the hands of Ira D. Sankey, that it received real publicity. As the authorship was unknown, the words were erroneously attributed to Dr. Horatius Bonar, and it was not until six or eight years after the hymn first appeared in Sankey's collection, that the true authorship was discovered; just a year or two before Mr. Scriven died. As many hundreds of thousands of copies must have been scattered throughout the world before the authorship was corrected, it is hardly to be wondered at, that even after the passing of fifty years, Dr. Bonar's name is still to be found appearing over "What a Friend we have in Jesus," as may be observed in a hymn book of considerable influence, published within the last year or two.

The simple but pleasing melody by which it is still sung, was written by Dr. C. C. Converse, a noted American composer, soon after the verses first appeared in print.

HUGH STOWELL.

ANOTHER Hymn, reminiscent of the "blessed hour of prayer," which breathes peace and consolation, is the one beginning:

> From every stormy wind that blows,
> From every swelling tide that flows,
> There is a calm, a safe retreat;
> 'Tis found beneath the Mercy-seat.
>
> There is a spot where spirits blend,
> Where friend holds fellowship with friend;
> Though sundered far, by faith we meet
> Around one common Mercy-seat.

This hymn first appeared in print just over a hundred years ago; but a few years later, in 1831, it was re-written, and the revised form, which was at once adopted by hymnal editors, has since been extensively used in practically all English-speaking countries.

Hugh Stowell, the author of this hymn, was a Church of England Vicar, who, in his day, bore a high reputation as a faithful and zealous preacher of the Gospel. He was born at Douglas, Isle of Man, in 1799. The greater part of his life was spent at Salford, across the river from Manchester, where he gathered multitudes to hear the Gospel. Here he preached with such power and fervour to the people who thronged to his services, that a larger and more commodious church had to be built, the entire cost of which, was willingly met by the generosity of his congregation. Though he laboured with but one thought, and that, the spiritual welfare of the flock committed to his charge, it would appear that the remarkable results of his untiring labours, did not pass unnoticed by the ecclesiastical dignitaries of that diocese, for about this time he was appointed an honorary Canon of Chester Cathedral, and later became rural Dean of Salford. "The duty of these deans," says one writer, "is to do their best to keep the bishops out of their cathedrals." Certainly Canon Stowell was no lover of ritualism for his sympathies all ran toward the Low Church and evangelical wing of the Anglican Communion.

Hugh Stowell was not only a popular and effective preacher, but was a writer of some note. After his death at Salford, in 1865, a small volume containing several of his sermons and forty-six of his hymns was published. From this collection, besides the hymn already quoted, our assembly hymn book compilers have chosen one of Stowell's best known compositions:

> Jesus is our Shepherd, wiping every tear,
> Folded in His bosom, what have we to fear?
> Only let us follow whither He doth lead,
> To the thirsty desert or the dewy mead.

This hymn was written as a Sunday School anniversary hymn in 1849, and very soon came into popular favour. Though primarily written for children, "Jesus is our Shepherd" has a general application, and, indeed, is very largely used as having such. There is a note of tenderness in the second stanza:

> Jesus is our Shepherd, well we know His voice!
> How its gentlest whisper makes our heart rejoice:
> Even when He chideth, tender is its tone;
> None but He shall guide us; we are His alone.

It is not surprising to learn that the author of "From every stormy wind that blows," the hymn by which Hugh Stowell is best known, was pre-eminently a man of prayer. "My father's last utterances," writes his son, "abundantly showed his love of, and delight in prayer, couched for the most part in the language of Holy Scripture, and these prayers were characterised by the deepest humility and most entire self-distrust. Equally apparent was his simple and firm reliance on his Saviour. To the question, "Is Jesus with you and precious to you?" the answer was, "Yes, so that He is all and in all to me." His was indeed "The calm, the safe retreat," of which he has sung.

SAMUEL P. TREGELLES.

Holy Saviour! we adore Thee,
　　Seated on the throne of God;
While the heavenly hosts before Thee
　　Gladly sing Thy praise aloud,
　　　　Thou art worthy!
　　We are ransomed by Thy blood.

SAMUEL P. TREGELLES, the author of the hymn of which the opening verse is given, ranks among the minor hymn writers of the early Brethren. The son of a Quaker, he was born at Falmouth, Cornwall, in January, 1813, and was educated at the Grammar School there. Converted in his youth, Tregelles, at an early age associated himself with Brethren. For some time he was a private tutor, but his keen interest in Biblical studies led him to devote the greater part of his life to the collation of ancient manuscripts of the New Testament. The first specimens of his laborious task were published in 1838, and five years later there appeared the first instalment of his Greek New Testament, completed, at long intervals, but not before the constant strain of many years' strenuous labour had ruined his health and reduced him to straightened circumstances. Stricken with paralysis, the progress of his work was hindered, and had to be completed by his friend and fellow helper B. W. Newton.

In pursuance of his studies, Dr. Tregelles visited Rome and spent much time and made critical research among many ancient documents. He was one of the most distinguished Biblical scholars of his day.

In recognition of his able theological work, Dr. Tregelles received a Civil List Pension. He was one of the revisers of the New Testament, but continued ill-health prevented him exercising his profound Biblical knowledge, and he was compelled to retire from taking further active part in this important work.

In his early years Dr. Tregelles was in fellowship with believers meeting at that time in Rawstorne Street, Camden Town, London; but in later years, owing to the unhappy strife that arose over the ideas propounded by B. W. Newton, he reluctantly severed his connection with the Brethren, and entered the Church of England. He died at Plymouth, April 24th, 1875.

Samuel P. Tregelles began writing hymns when he was about twenty-four, and continued at intervals till a few years before his death. One of his earliest compositions, written about 1838, which is still in general use, begins:

> Thy Name we bless, Lord Jesus!
> That Name all names excelling:
> How great Thy love, all praise above,
>   Should every tongue be telling.
> The Father's loving-kindness
>   In giving Thee was shown us;
> Now by Thy blood, redeemed to God,
>   As children He doth own us.

HYMNS AND THEIR WRITERS. 79

His long and intimate connection with Brethren secured for Tregelles a position in their midst as a hymn writer, and practically all his compositions made their first appearance in "Hymns for the Poor of the Flock," and other similar hymnals published since that time.

The hymns of Tregelles are in use almost exclusively amongst Brethren, and as one might be led to expect, they are characterised by a high spiritual tone; but taken generally, the hymns from his pen do not approach the distinctive merit attained by many of his contemporaries.

Besides the hymns quoted, he is the author of "Father! we, Thy children, bless Thee," and "Thy broken body, gracious Lord." Amongst the last hymns written by Dr. Tregelles is the one beginning:

> Lord Jesus, we believing
> In Thee have peace with God,
> Eternal life receiving,
> The purchase of Thy blood.
> Our curse and condemnation
> Thou bearest in our stead;
> Secure is our salvation
> In Thee, our risen Head.

T. R. TAYLOR.

AMONGST writers in the various hymn books from whose compositions but a single hymn has been chosen, the name of T. R. Taylor is almost passed by. But if the name of the author is unfamiliar, not so the hymn; for very few heavenly songs possess the charm and beauty of:

> I'm but a stranger here—
> Heaven is my home;
> Earth is a desert drear—
> Heaven is my home;
> Danger and sorrow stand
> Round me on every hand,
> Heaven is my Fatherland—
> Heaven is my home.

There is a touch of pathos added when we remember that this beautiful and affecting hymn was written during the author's last illness. Thomas Ranson Taylor was the grandson of a Northumberland farmer. His father was a dissenting minister at the Yorkshire village of Ossett, and it was here that the author was born on May 9th, 1807. The year following, his father removed to Bradford to take charge of a large Congregational Church. At the age of fifteen the lad worked as clerk in a merchant's office, but was afterwards apprenticed to Mr. Dunn, a printer, who seems to have been a person of high Christian character. Under his godly care the lad grew up into a promising young man, and influenced by intense religious desires, he left the printing office to enter Airedale Independent College to prepare for the ministry. His first and only charge was Howard Street Chapel, Sheffield, where, during his brief ministry, he attracted the attention of James Montgomery, who gave him much encour-

HYMNS AND THEIR WRITERS.

agement, not only in his ministerial duties, but also in his poetical pursuits.

His health was not robust, and he soon developed symptoms of serious lung trouble, which constantly interrupted his preaching, and he was obliged to relinquish his charge after a brief service of only six months.

Returning to Bradford, he assisted his father and for a short time acted as classical tutor at Airedale College, where he had formerly sat as a student; but his strength gradually failed, and he passed to the home of which he sang, on March 15th, 1835, in his 29th year.

Thomas Ranson Taylor is the author of several poems and a few hymns, but his best known work is "I'm but a stranger here," which was originally set to the plaintive air, "Robin Adair," to which it is still frequently sung.

The closing stanza strikes a tender note, as in thought, the weary pilgrim halts on the way to look across the "narrow sea," and as he views the home beyond, gives expression to the deep longing of the heart in the lines:

> There, at my Saviour's side—
> Heaven is my home;
> I shall be glorified—
> Heaven is my home;
> There, with the good and blest,
> Those I loved most and best,
> I shall for ever rest—
> Heaven is my home.

HORATIUS BONAR.

> I heard the voice of Jesus say,
> "Come unto Me and rest;
> Lay down, thou weary one, lay down
> Thy head upon My breast."

HAD Dr. Bonar written no other hymn than "I heard the voice of Jesus say," the great hymnist, by this one composition, would have bestowed on posterity a gem of sacred song, willed of God to be used in bringing peace and consolation to countless thousands the world over.

The most eminent of all Scottish hymn writers, and well to the forefront of the world's hymnists of last century, the name of Dr. Horatius Bonar may well rank with Watts, Doddridge and Wesley. His hymns, simple enough that a child can understand, yet profoundly spiritual withal, are loved and sung, not only in the land that gave him birth, but in countries beyond the seas, wherever these heavenly songs have been carried. Horatius Bonar was the son of a lawyer, and was born in Edinburgh on December 19th, 1808. He was one of several brothers who all became eminent ministers in the Church of Scotland. Educated at the famous High School and University of his native city, in his student days he came under the influence of such men as Dr. Chalmers, Edward Irving and Robert Murray McCheyne. He early decided to devote his life to the Lord's service in the ministry of the Gospel, and on completing his theological course he undertook mission work at St John's Church, Leith. It was here that he began to write hymns. Keenly interested in young folks, the Sunday School, under his care very quickly grew and prospered. When he first began mission work, he found the boys and girls listless

HYMNS AND THEIR WRITERS.

and indifferent in the matter of public worship. Accustomed to the use of psalms, not exactly suited, either in word or tune, to meet the needs of the young folks, Mr. Bonar realised that what ought to have been the brightest part of the services, was to them the dullest. And yet the children loved music, and were ready enough to sing songs on week days. So he tried an experiment. Choosing a few familiar tunes such as "The Flowers of the Forest," he set to work writing words to them. These he had printed in leaflet form and distributed amongst the young folks in the Sunday School. To Mr. Bonar's delight the experiment succeeded, and the children immediately took to singing the new hymns which had been specially written for them. In this way were written Horatius Bonar's first two hymns—"I lay my sins on Jesus," and "The morning, the bright and the beautiful morning."

After four-and-a-half years' work at Leith he became minister of the North Parish Church, Kelso, in November, 1837, where he laboured with a devotion and enthusiasm that never waned during his long and faithful ministry. His first sermon was long remembered by those who heard it delivered from the pulpit. It was a clarion call to prayer. "Pray brethren!" was his cry, "so shall the showers of heaven descend upon our church, our parish, our schools, our families. It is to prayer I urge you, to prayer for yourselves, to prayer for me!" But Horatius Bonar was pre-eminently a man of prayer, and in after years, the voice of earnest pleading from behind the fast-closed door of his study, pleading that continued often for hours at a time, formed one of the most sacred memories in his own home circle.

Strong physically, Dr. Bonar was never idle.

At Kelso, it is said, that, in one day, he frequently preached three times in the pulpit and once in the open-air. He was a valiant for the Truth, and even as an old man, when at Edinburgh, his stentorian voice could be heard heralding forth the Gospel in the open-air, sometimes in the Meadows and sometimes in Parliament Square. One friend said of him that he was always preaching, another that he was always visiting, another that he was always writing, and yet another that he was always praying.

At the Disruption of 1843, Dr. Bonar remained at Kelso as minister of the Free Church of Scotland, and it was here that most of his best known hymns were written, including "I heard the voice of Jesus say," which is perhaps the most loved of all his compositions.

In 1866, Dr. Bonar removed to Edinburgh, the place of his birth, where he undertook the charge of a new church. Here he laboured till he was past eighty, and though the press of city work somewhat retarded the outpouring of hymns, yet his pen was never still. For a time he edited two magazines and was, in addition, continually publishing prose works. He was also the author of hundreds of tracts, one of which, "Believe and Live," published in 1839, reached a circulation of a million copies.

The visit to Scotland of Moody and Sankey in 1873-74, seemed to revive the flow of hymns, and about this time fresh compositions began to appear in his notebooks, many of these specially written for Mr. Sankey. Regarding one hymn written about this time, there is an interesting story. Mr. Sankey had been singing Tennyson's sad and beautiful poem, "Late, late, so late, and dark the night and chill," for which he had com-

Yours truly,
Horatius Bonar

posed a tune. On asking permission of the owner of the copyright to use it in his collection of hymns, he was refused. So, being left with a tune without the words, Sankey requested Dr. Bonar to write a hymn which would convey the same scriptural theme. This was done, and the now well-known hymn, "Yet there is room," was the result.

An outstanding feature of the hymns of this notable Scottish Presbyterian is that they belong to no particular denomination, but are in use in almost every form of Christian worship, wherever the songs of Zion are sung. Dr. Bonar wrote about 600 hymns—not including sixty translations of different Psalms—and these are to be found in hymnals the world over. Possibly the best known are:—"I heard the voice of Jesus say," "I lay my sins on Jesus," "Thy way not mine, O Lord," "I was a wandering sheep," "A few more years shall roll," "Here, O my Lord, I see Thee face to face." His own favourite was—

> When the weary, seeking rest,
> To Thy goodness flee.

Besides those already mentioned, such hymns as the following have gained much favour:— "Blessed be God our God," "Done is the work that saves," "For the bread and for the wine," and that inspiring song of worship and thanksgiving:—

> No blood, no altar now,
>   The sacrifice is o'er!
> No flame, no smoke ascends on high,
>   The lamb is slain no more.
> But richer blood has flow'd from nobler veins,
> To purge the soul from guilt, and cleanse the reddest stains.

Appropriate in closing are the words taken from his Pilgrim Song:

> A few more suns shall set
> O'er time's dark hills of time,
> And we shall be where suns are not,
> A far serener clime.

After a lingering illness, borne with Christian fortitude, his last sun set on July 31st, 1889, and Dr. Horatius Bonar passed to that serener clime of which he sang: into the presence of the King.

ROBERT C. CHAPMAN.

> O my Saviour, crucified,
> Near Thy cross would I abide,
> There to look with steadfast eye
> On Thy dying agony.

FEW adoration hymns have been penned with more thoughtful care, than the one of which we give the opening stanza. Breathing words of peace and love in every line, it forms a wonderful pen-picture, carrying our thoughts in a peculiar way from earth's cold vale, to the calm of Calvary's brow. This gem of sacred verse, is one of the many devotional hymns written by Robert Cleaver Chapman, the Barnstaple patriarch. Born in Denmark on January 4th, 1803, where his parents had gone to live, he had the inestimable advantage of being brought up under the constant care and guidance of a godly mother, who not only stored his young mind with Scripture, but undertook the task of giving the boy such tuition that she was able, till he was about nine or ten years old. He was sent to England to complete His education and very soon gave evidence of a remarkable proficiency in literature, which particular study he determined to take up as a profession. Mr. Chapman's plans were changed, however, and he studied law, subsequently becoming a solicitor, in which pursuit he very soon attained to a good position. When he was in his twentieth year, Mr. Chapman—who was at that time residing in London—came under the influence of the gifted preacher, James Harrington Evans, when he underwent a great spiritual change.

He at once took a decided stand as a follower of the Lord Jesus Christ, and having made a public confession of his faith by following the Lord through the waters of baptism, he associated himself with those Christians who were faithful to the teaching of God's Word. In course of time Mr. Chapman felt called of God to relinquish his profession and give himself entirely to the ministry of the Word. When advised by his friends to reconsider his decision, for, said they, he would never make a preacher. Mr. Chapman characteristically replied, "There are many who preach Christ, but not so many who live Christ; my great aim will be to live Christ." In the year 1832 he removed to Barnstaple, a place which will always be fragrant with cherished memories of this saintly man.

"In the very year that Robert Chapman took up his residence at Barnstaple, with the steadfast purpose of seeking to learn and carry out all the will of God, George Muller and his friend and fellow-labourer, Henry Craik, took up their abode in Bristol. These servants of Christ had already been exercised about many things at Teignmouth, and on the evening of the 13th August, at Bethesda Chapel, Mr. Muller, Mr. Craik, one other brother, and four sisters (only seven in all) sat down together, uniting in Church fellowship, 'without any rules, desiring to act only as the Lord should be pleased to give light through His Word.'"

It will be remembered that it was about this particular period that a number of the Lord's children in Dublin and other places, had been similarly guided in following the principles laid down in God's Word. Thus, when in due course, they came together, it was found that in many respects they were of one mind as to the true interpretation of the Scriptures regarding the fellowship of saints.

A true and valiant witness for God throughout a long and useful life, the honoured name of Robert Cleaver Chapman is so well-known to readers that it would be superfluous to write at any great length here.

On the evening of June 12th, 1902, he passed into the presence of the King in his 100th year.

Mr. Chapman ranks amongst the comparatively few hymn writers of repute whose hymns were composed almost exclusively for the use of believers in connection with the various assemblies. In 1837 he published a collection, "Hymns for use of the Church of Christ," which was reprinted fifteen years later. Mr. Chapman's hymns and poems number about 165, most of which are to be found in his "Hymns and Meditations," published in 1871.

A communion hymn of rare beauty, based on the text, "This do in remembrance of Me, begins:

> With Jesus in our midst
> We gather round the board;
> Though many, we are one in Christ,
> One body in the Lord.

ROBERT CLEAVER CHAPMAN.

JOHN NELSON DARBY.

HYMNS AND THEIR WRITERS. 89

A hymn which strikes a singularly triumphant note, and is appropriately set to the tune of Luther's hymn is:

> The Lord of Glory! Who is He?
> Who is the King of Glory?
> Only the Son of God can be
> The Christ, the King of Glory.
> Consider all His wounds, and see
> How Jesus' death upon the tree
> Proclaims Him King of Glory.

Mr. Chapman is also the author of "The Lamb of God to slaughter led," "Jesus, in His Heavenly Temple," "No bone of Thee was broken," and that much loved hymn, which is a good example of its author's poetic power:

> No condemnation! O my soul,
> 'Tis God that speaks the word;
> Perfect in comliness art Thou
> In Christ thy glorious Lord.

The sweet melody "Orlington," where the words of the third line in each verse are repeated, makes a very fitting tune for this hymn. Mr. Chapman had a ready pen and was a valuable contributor to various periodicals for Christians. His books include, "Seventy Years of Pilgrimage," "Choice Sayings," "Precious Portions," and "Hymns and Meditations." Though it is chiefly as a minister of God's Word that the name of Robert Chapman will best be remembered, yet, the poetic tendencies of his genius as a writer of devotional hymns, has secured for him a niche in the hearts of believers, not only in our own but other countries.

J. DENHAM SMITH.

My God, I have found
The thrice blessed ground,
Where life, and where joy,
And true comfort abound.
Hallelujah! Thine the glory!
Hallelujah! Amen!
Hallelujah! Thine the glory!
Revive me again!

A REVIVAL hymn, which strikes an exultant note, giving fervent expression to the pent up aspirations, not only in the heart of the young believer in the ecstasy of his new found joy, but to weary travellers along life's pilgrimage journey, it comes with a power and freshness, reviving memories of that "Happy day" that fixed our choice.

The writer of this hymn is Joseph Denham Smith. Formerly a Congregational Minister, he was mightily used of God in Ireland during the '59 Revival, and the years which followed that remarkable wave of spiritual blessing.

He was born in 1817, at Romsey, Hants., where he spent his childhood. Tenderly watched over by his widowed mother, who ceased not to pray for the conversion of her boy to God, he was led to the Saviour at an early age, and by the time he had reached his sixteenth year he was preaching the Gospel. After studying for some time at the Dublin Theological Institute, he entered the Congregational Ministry in 1840. Nine years later Mr. Denham Smith removed to Kingstown, where he assiduously devoted himself to the pastorage of the Congregational Church of that town, an association destined of God in opening up a wide field for evangelistic work, the fruits of which, after the passing of more than half a century, are apparent to-day.

It was in 1859, when Northern Ireland, aflame with the fires of a mighty revival, that Mr. Denham Smith, impelled by a loving desire, and a yearning for souls, responded to the call of the Lord, and left his church for Dublin, where he engaged one of the largest halls in the city. Here, with the help of friends of like mind, he commenced evangelistic services such as had never before been known in the Irish capital. It is said that "thousands flocked together in the morning, and remained hour after hour—many without refreshments—until ten and eleven at night. Careless ones were awakened, anxious ones led into peace, and persons of all classes rejoiced in a newly-found Saviour."

The outcome of this remarkable work, so manifestly owned of God, was the erection of the well-known Merrion Hall, Dublin, which has since been used for the proclamation of the Gospel, and is a noted centre where believers from many parts gather for the faithful ministry and exposition of God's Word.

After a visit to the Continent, where largely-attended meetings were held in Paris and Geneva, Mr. Denham Smith returned to England, and finally settled in London. Here he enjoyed the warm fellowship of Dr Habershon—father of Ada R. Habershon, the writer of many of Charles M. Alexander's new hymns. It was through his kindly interest that St. George's Hall was engaged for Sunday services, thus opening up the way for Mr. Smith's evangelistic work in the Metropolis. He afterwards preached in many of the large halls in the city, and finally continued to minister regularly in St. George's Hall.

Possessed of a remarkable eloquence, Mr. Denham Smith, whether preaching the Gospel or expounding the Scriptures, never failed to at once arrest the attention of his hearers. He was a great lover of hymns and hymn singing. Writing of these days, when Mr. Smith became a frequent visitor to the home of Dr. Habershon his devoted friend, Miss Habershon says: "It was his delightful custom when in London to call at Brook Street on Monday afternoons, and I think scarcely a visit passed without our gathering with him round the piano to sing some of his favourite hymns. He had a beautiful tenor voice, and it was always a pleasure to hear him taking his part."

Mr. Denham Smith's evangelistic work both in England and Ireland will long be remembered, and in this connection he published a considerable number of tracts and pamphlets which had a large circulation. During the Revival he issued a hymn book called "Times of Refreshing," containing many of his own compositions which had been sung during those stirring times, and had now become general favourites among mission workers. An enlarged edition was brought out in 1885. This collection gave evidence of the compiler's judicious care in using only such hymns that were free of doubtful theology. In the compiling of his hymn book, Mr. Denham Smith proved himself a keen and able hymnologist. At all times, says one who assisted in this work, his conversation was of itself edifying and instructive, for he gave much thought to each hymn, being careful as to arrangement according to the subject in each particular case.

It was about the year 1860 that J. Denham Smith wrote his best known hymn:

> Just as Thou art—how wondrous fair,
> Lord Jesus, all Thy members are,
> A life divine to them is given—
> A long inheritance in heaven.

HYMNS AND THEIR WRITERS. 93

> Just as Thou art—nor doubt, nor fear
> Can with Thy spotlessness appear;
> O timeless love! as Thee I'm seen
> The righteousness of God in Him.

He was not a prolific hymn writer, nor are his compositions greatly known outside a rather limited circle. Nevertheless his hymns ring true, and there are many of them of no mean merit, which are deserving of a wider circulation. Especially is this so in the case of the inspiring hymn, beginning:

> Rise, my soul! behold 'tis Jesus,
> Jesus fills thy wondering eyes;
> See Him now in glory seated,
> Where thy sins no more can rise.

Another of equal merit, which speaks peace to the heart of the child of God, and strikes a joyous note of assurance, telling of a Father's love and tender care for His own, is the hymn:

> God's almighty arms are round me,
> Peace, peace, is mine!
> Judgment scenes need not confound me,
> Peace, peace, is mine!
> Jesus came Himself and sought me;
> Sold to death He found and bought me;
> Then my blessed freedom taught me,
> Peace, peace, is mine.

After a fruitful ministry extending over fifty years, during which time he had endeared himself to all with whom he came in contact, Mr. J. Denham Smith passed into the presence of the King, in the Spring of 1889, and was laid to rest in West Hamstead Cemetery, London.

SAMUEL TREVOR FRANCIS.

> I am waiting for the dawning
> Of the bright and blessed day,
> When the darksome night of sorrow
> Shall have vanished far away;
> When for ever with the Saviour,
> Far beyond this vale of tears,
> I shall swell the song of worship
> Through the everlasting years.

SAMUEL TREVOR FRANCIS has contributed comparatively few hymns to present-day collections, but each of his hymns may be said to be of outstanding merit. One composition of which the opening verse is here given, is a hymn of great beauty, exulting in the joyous anticipation of the coming again of our Lord and Saviour Jesus Christ. Appropriately set to one of Haydn's musical compositions, rather suggests that the writer, in forming his verses, used this easy flowing melody as a vehicle to give expression to this ever-absorbing theme. This is particularly noticable in the seventh line of each verse, where the music spontaneously swells out, exactly suiting the thought conveyed by the writer. The origin of this well-known tune is interesting. Haydn went to Austria during a time of famine, and as he sat in the hotel at which he was staying, there was borne to him from the public square some distance away, where the famished people had gathered to receive food, the long, mournful wail of peasants, followed by the loud, exultant notes of joy as the officials appeared with supplies of bread. Putting the two together, Haydn composed the melody known as "The Austrian Air," so eminently suited to "I am waiting for the dawning."

Another hymn by Mr. Francis is one of tender adoration:

> Saviour, we remember Thee!
> Thy deep woe and agony,
> All Thy suffering on the tree,
> Saviour, we adore Thee!

Samuel Trevor Francis was born at Cheshunt, Herts., November 19th, 1834, and when yet a child was taken to Hull. As he grew into boyhood he came under the sweet influence of a godly grandmother, who taught the boy his letters, the principal reading book being the Bible.

"One of my earliest recollections," once wrote Mr. Trevor, "is going with my eldest brother into my mother's room, and made to kneel with her, while she poured out her soul in earnest supplication that her boys might grow up to be God-fearing men."

When little more than a boy, Samuel began to put together rhymes, which were scribbled for his own and his friends amusement. His little poems, however, showed unmistakable signs of the poetic propensity which only waited for future development. Before Samuel Francis had quite reached the years of youth, he gathered together his various compositions which had by this time accumulated, and copied them into a manuscript book of his own making. This book, however, he destroyed in a fit of irritation brought about by his eldest brother, who, jealous of the attention paid to these juvenile efforts, persistently annoyed and persecuted the youthful poet, with the result that, picking up the book containing his cherished effusions, he tore it from cover to cover. Thus many of his earliest poems were irretrievably lost.

The family having removed to London, it was designed that Samuel Francis should follow the medical profession. With this object in view he studied for about twelve months, but on the death of his father, the plans for his future career had to be altered. It was about this time that he became deeply concerned about his soul's eternal welfare, and on occasions he found himself crying to God for pardon and peace. Coming in contact with a prominent business man, a faithful servant of God, who gave most of his spare time for the spiritual welfare of young men, young Francis felt the burden of sin increase more than ever. But there came a climax. "I was on my way home from work," he said when recounting the story, "and had to cross Hungerford Bridge to the south of the Thames. It was a winter's night of wind and rain, and in the loneliness of that walk I cried to God to have mercy upon me. Staying for a moment to look at the dark waters flowing under the bridge, the temptation was whispered to me, 'Make an end of all this misery.' I drew back from the evil thought, and suddenly a message was borne into my very soul, 'You do believe on the Lord Jesus Christ?' I at once answered, 'I do believe,' and I put my whole trust in Him as my Saviour. Instantly there came this reply, 'Then you are saved!' and with a thrill of joy I ran across the bridge, burst through the turnstile, and pursued my way home, repeating the words again and again, 'Then I am saved! then I am saved!'"

Mr. Francis early associated himself with the assembly of believers meeting at Kennington, which was but the first stepping-stone towards the various services in the Lord's work in which he showed a never-failing interest during his long and useful life.

As a singer of the Gospel Mr. Francis was much used of God, and during the memorable Moody and Sankey mission, when a great wave of spiritual revival swept over these islands, he greatly assisted

HYMNS AND THEIR WRITERS.

in the musical part of the services held in the Agricultural Hall, London, where, on several occasions he acted as Mr. Sankey's deputy.

The poems and hymns of S. Trevor Francis were collected and published in book form, after the author had passed three-score years and ten. A hymn, which already appears in one or two collections, ranks among his best, and is worthy of a place in every hymnal. Here is the opening verse:

> O the deep, deep love of Jesus
> Vast, unmeasured, boundless, free;
> Rolling as a mighty ocean
> In its fulness over me!
> Underneath me, all around me,
> Is the current of Thy love,
> Leading onward, leading homeward,
> To my glorious rest above.

On December 28th, 1925, S. Trevor Francis entered the glorious rest above, of which he loved to sing, at the advanced age of ninety-one.

EDWARD H. BICKERSTETH.

> "Till He come!" O let the words
> Linger on the trembling chords;
> Let the "little while" between
> In their golden light be seen;
> Let us think how heaven and home
> Lie beyond that "Till He come!"

DR. Edward H. Bickersteth, the author of this hymn, was a voluminous writer of sacred songs, and a notable leader of evangelical thought, as his various compositions unmistakably reveal. Written in 1861, "Till He come" was the outcome of an earnest desire on the part of the author to enforce the words of Scripture, "Ye do shew the Lord's death till He come," an aspect of the Lord's Supper which he considered had been passed over in many church hymnals in use at that time.

The verse which particularly dwells on the feast of remembrance, reminiscent of a time so precious to the child of God, is:

> See, the feast of love is spread!
> Drink the wine, and break the bread:
> Sweet memorials, till the Lord
> Calls us round His heavenly board;
> Some from earth, from glory some,
> Severed only "Till He come!"

Dr. Bickersteth was the son of Edward Bickersteth who wrote the hymn "Light of the world"; and was born at Islington, London, on January 26th, 1825. He was educated at Trinity College, Cambridge, where his poetic gifts obtained for him high honours,

Entering the Church of England, he received his first curacy at Bannington, Norfolk, and after a notable career, was appointed Bishop of Exeter in 1885. Dr. Bickersteth took an active interest in missionary work, giving not only his time and substance but also his son Edward, who died in the foreign field.

"As a poet, Dr. Bickersteth is well-known," says Dr. Julian, the noted hymnologist, "his reputation as a hymn writer has also extended far and wide. Joined with a strong grasp of his subject, true poetic feeling, a pure rhythm, there is a soothing plaintiveness and individuality in his hymns, which give them a distinct character of their own."

It is, however, as the author of one outstanding composition that his fame as a hymn writer rests: a lyric of surpassing charm and beauty:

> Peace, perfect peace, in this dark world of sin,
> The blood of Jesus whispers peace within.
>
> Peace, perfect peace, with sorrows surging round,
> On Jesus' bosom, nought but calm is found.

This hymn was written at Harrogate in a house facing the Stray, in August, 1875. It is said that Dr. Bickersteth received the inspiration to pen the verses after hearing a sermon preached from the text: "Thou wilt keep him in perfect peace, whose mind is stayed on Thee."

The evening of a long and useful life was spent in peaceful retirement, and, on the morning of May 16th, 1906, from his residence at Paddington, London, Dr. Edward H. Bickersteth passed into the presence of the Lord.

It will have been observed that many standard English hymns, familiar to the reader, have not been referred to. This has not been an oversight, these having been fully dealt with elsewhere by the present writer.† The object of this volume is to refer only to the hymns in general use amongst the various assemblies of the Lord's people, known as the Brethren.

† "The Romance of Sacred Song."

HENRY F. LYTE.

ALTHOUGH Henry F. Lyte is immortalised by "Abide with me," he is the author of many other hymns. A composition of his, which breathes the language of the pilgrim whose heart longs for the glories above, is fitly expressed in the hymn which opens:

> My rest is in heaven, my rest is not here,
> Then why should I murmur when trials are near?
> Be hushed, my sad spirit, the worst that can come
> But shortens the journey and hastens me home.

Henry Francis Lyte was born at the village of Ednam on the Scottish Border, on June 1st, 1793. He was intended for the medical profession, but the plans of his parents were changed, and Henry entered the Church of England, his first curacy being at Tagmon, County Wexford. Here the young minister preached about three years before he was converted. The great spiritual change took place when visiting a neighbouring clergyman, one of his most intimate friends, who lay dying. The sick man intimated to his friend that he feared he was not prepared to meet God. This aroused Lyte to the realization of his own lost condition, and together they read the Scriptures, not in the formal manner as had been their custom, but in anxiety of heart in search of light. The result was that both found the way of salvation through the finished work of the Cross. "My friend," says Lyte, "died happy in the belief that, though he had greatly sinned, there was One whose death and sufferings had atoned for his iniquities, and that he was forgiven and accepted for His sake." Henry Lyte was then just twenty-five. From this time onward he was a changed man, and began to study the Bible, and to preach in an altogether different manner than he had previously done.

He removed to Brixham, a fishing village on the Devonshire coast, where for twenty-five years, despite incessant ill-health, he laboured devotedly as a faithful servant of Christ, ministering to the needs of the rough yet warm-hearted fisher folks. It was here that "Abide with me," possibly his last hymn, was written. Worn out by work and anxiety, Lyte became seriously ill, and was ordered abroad to a sunnier clime. Before leaving his beloved flock, to whom he was greatly attached, Lyte preached a farewell sermon in which he tenderly besought his hearers to "seek the Lord while He may be found," emphasising the all-importance of salvation through the precious blood of Christ. He got through the service with difficulty, and after wandering for a short time in the garden of his home at Berry Head, he sought the quietude of his room, and throwing himself on the couch, found solace for his mind and heart by composing one of the sweetest hymns in the English language:

> Abide with me: fast falls the eventide;
> The darkness deepens; Lord with me abide:
> While other helpers fail, and comforts flee,
> Help of the helpless, O abide with me!
>
> Swift to its close ebbs out life's little day;
> Earth's joys grow dim, its glories pass away;
> Change and decay in all around I see;
> O Thou, who changest not, abide with me!

The eventide of which he sang was indeed falling fast, for shortly after arriving at Nice, in the South of France, he died there, on November 20th, 1847.

REGINALD HEBER.

> From Greenland's icy mountains,
> From India's coral strand,
> Where Africa's sunny fountains
> Roll down their golden sand;
> From many an ancient river,
> From many a palmy plain,
> They call us to deliver
> Their land from error's chain.

OF all missionary hymns few have attained such a measure of unbounded favour, almost since its birth over a hundred years ago, as that bestowed upon "From Greenland's Icy Mountains." It was written in less than half-an-hour, to meet a temporary need. And little did Reginald Heber realise as he hurriedly penned the lines one Saturday night, away back in 1819, that the hymn would not only be sung at the missionary service, to be held in the ancient North Wales Church of Wrexham the day following, but would live to be sung the world over.

Reginald Heber was on a visit to his father-in-law, Dr. Shipley, vicar of Wrexham, who had to preach a sermon on the following day in aid of the Society for the Propagation of the Gospel in foreign parts. At a loss for a suitable hymn, he turned to Heber and asked if he would write something appropriate for the occasion. His son-in-law went over to a side table, and in a short time returned with the hymn now so well-known.

These were the days when the duty of the worthy precentor was to first read aloud a line or two of the hymn, which was afterwards sung by the congregation to some familiar melody. On this occasion, it is said that "From Greenland's Icy Mountains" was sung to an old ballad tune.

The beautiful melody to which the hymn is now universally sung has an equally romantic

HYMNS AND THEIR WRITERS. 103

origin. About four years after the hymn was written, a copy was sent to a lady residing at Savannah, in the Southern State of Georgia, America. Arrested by its beauty, and at once realising its power as a missionary hymn, she sought for a tune to fit the words, but the metre 7.6.7.6.D being little known at this time, she was unable to find a measure to suit. A few doors along the street there lived a young bank clerk who was known to have the gift of composing tunes, and she sent a boy with the verses and a request that he might write a new tune. In an incredibly short time the boy returned with the now famous tune "Heber." The young bank clerk whose early musical effort was willed to share equal honours with Reginald Heber's now famous hymn, became the celebrated composer, Dr. Lowell Mason.

Heber was born in 1783, and after a distinguished career at Oxford, he entered the ministry of the Church of England. At the age of forty he was appointed Bishop of Calcutta, but after a brief service of three years in the foreign field, he died suddenly from apoplexy, in the midst of his labours, on April 3rd, 1826.

Under date of September, 1823—the year he sailed to India—there is an interesting reference in his diary to the lines:

> What though the spicy breezes
> Blow soft o'er Ceylon's Isle.

"Though we are too far off Ceylon to catch the odours of the land," he writes, "yet it is, we are assured, perfectly true that such odours are perceptible to a very considerable distance. In the Straits of Malacca a smell like that of hawthorn hedge is commonly experienced; and from Ceylon, at thirty or forty miles, under certain circumstances, a yet more agreeable scent is inhaled."

Though "From Greenland's Icy Mountains" is a striking example of spontaneous writing, it is remarkable that the only correction the author ever made was in the second verse, where he substituted the word "heathen" for that of "savage."

ALBERT MIDLANE.

"Revive Thy work, O Lord!"
Thy mighty arm make bare;
Speak with the voice which wakes the dead,
And make Thy people hear.

IN these days, when, from time to time there is wafted to us on the gentle winds of hope, whispers of a coming Revival, our whole spiritual being, expectant and alert, involuntarily rises to the joyful sound, as there bursts forth from the heart, the one passionate prayer, so powerfully presented and expressed in these inspiring lines.

The author of this universally popular hymn is Albert Midlane. He was born at Newport, Isle of Wight, on January 23rd, 1825, three months after the death of his father. He had the inestimable privilege of a godly mother, who watched over her fatherless boy with a tender and loving care, which she unselfishly bestowed until the future hymn writer was well into manhood. In after years Mr. Midlane related how he remembered his mother saying, when at that time he could hardly take in the meaning of the words, "They told me when your father died that my

HYMNS AND THEIR WRITERS.

child would be the Lord's gift to cheer and help me in my widowhood." At the close of her life, fifty years later, the aged saint was able to thank the great Giver that the prediction had indeed come true.

Mr. Midlane took to writing hymns when little more than a boy, his first attempt being one for children, "God bless our Sunday School," which appeared in print when the author was still in his teens. In his boyhood days he was brought into close touch with Thomas Binnie, who wrote the well-known hymn "Eternal light, eternal light," from whom he may have received some encouragement and impetus in his poetical pursuits. In this connection, however, Mr. Midlane himself has said that it was his Sunday School teacher who did so much to shape his early life, and who prompted him to poetical efforts. The youthful poet would write his verses, and after the lessons were over, would show them to his teacher, a keen and enthusiastic student of poetry, who gave him valuable instruction.

Before he laid down his pen at the close of a long and useful life, Albert Midlane had written about a thousand hymns and poems. Amongst my hymnal treasures there is a long poem entitled "Eden Lost," written on a double sheet of foolscap. It is the original copy, penned by the hand of Albert Midlane in his later years, and bearing the signature of the noted hymn writer.

"Revive Thy work, O Lord," which is perhaps his second best known hymn, was first published in the "British Messenger," October 1858, and soon after appeared in a large number of hymnals in Great Britain and America. This hymn has been erroneously attributed to Fanny Crosby, the blind hymn writer. It appeared with her name, in a somewhat altered form in an American collection entitled "Brightest and Best," published in 1875, and afterwards in "Sankey's Sacred Songs and Solos," without reference to the real author. Dr. W. H. Doane, the noted composer, wrote the tune in Sankey's hymn book to which it is mostly sung, and has contributed in no small measure to the popularity of the hymn.

Besides "Revive Thy work, O Lord," other hymns, by Albert Midlane, familar to us, are "Without a cloud between," "Lord Jesus Thine," "Come, weary, anxious, laden soul," and:

> How vast, how full, how free,
> The mercy of our God!
> Proclaim the blessed news around,
> And spread it all abroad.

In the year 1861 Mr. Midlane wrote a hymn to be found in most mission hymnals in general use to-day. It is a hymn with no uncertain message, and strikes a direct note of warning and entreaty:

> Passing onward, quickly passing;
> But I ask thee, whither bound?
> Is it to the many mansions,
> Where eternal rest is found?
> Passing onward, passing onward,
> Tell me, sinner, whither bound?

It is, however, as the author of "There's a Friend for little Children" that the name of Albert Midlane has received a world-wide reputation. One of the most widely-known and best-loved of all children's hymns, this popular composition was written on February 27th, 1859, and first appeared in a children's periodical edited by his friend C. H. Mackintosh, under the title "Above the Bright blue Sky." The hymn at once attained great popularity. To-day it has found its way into almost every corner of the world, and has been translated into nearly fifty languages. Though

ALBERT MIDLANE.
Photograph taken two weeks before his home-call.

HYMNS AND THEIR WRITERS.

many long years have passed away since we first lisped these tender lines, the hymn has lost none of its old-time sweetness:

> There's a Friend for little children,
> Above the bright blue sky,
> A Friend that never changes,
> Whose love will never die;
> Unlike our friends by nature,
> Who change with changing years,
> This Friend is always worthy
> The precious name He bears.

A writer who was personally acquainted with the author of "There's a Friend for little Children," gives the following as the story of its origin: "Mr. Midlane's mind had been musing on its outline during the day, and in the evening, his family having retired to rest, he set himself to arrange and complete the idea. But time stole on, and morning came. Alarmed at his absence, his wife came downstairs, only to find her husband in a state of unconsciousness, with his head resting on the now finished hymn." The author had the pleasure of witnessing the celebration of the jubilee of his famous hymn, when 3,000 children assembled in St. Paul's Cathedral, London, joined in the singing of "There's a Friend for little Children."

Mr. Midlane was associated with Brethren from his early years, and was a familiar figure, not only in the corner of the Lord's vineyard where practically the whole of his life was spent, but also in assemblies further afield. When he had passed three-score years and ten, he gave this beautiful testimony: "Early brought to the Lord, and early devoted to His service, I have, through grace, been enabled to bear part in preaching the Gospel of God's grace and glory: as also in the continuous work of Sunday School labour; and thus it comes to pass that, at the age of seventy-five, I can almost say, like Moses, 'My eye is not dim, nor my natural force abated!' To Him, whose grace has been sufficient for me, be all the glory that, from seventeen to seventy-five, my mouth has been open to tell of His love, and my pen wielded to declare His praise!"

Considering his busy life in connection with an ironmongery business which he conducted, Mr. Midlane was a fairly voluminous writer. Though perhaps a few of his hymns may not manifest a particularly high degree of literary merit, nevertheless the tone is good, and there is an unmistakable loyalty to the Word of God, beautifully expressed, which, perhaps, in hymn writing, is of no inconsiderable importance.

Albert Midlane passed away on February 28th, 1909, and was laid to rest in Carisbrooke Cemetery.

ALEXANDER STEWART.

O Lamb of God! we lift our eyes
To Thee amidst the throne;
Shine on us, bid Thy light arise,
And make Thy glory known.

THERE are few songs of the sanctuary, reminiscent of sweet and precious moments spent in the presence of Him of whom it sings, than Alexander Stewart's choice hymn, the opening stanza of which is given above. The author of these lines, whose name is still a fragrant memory, not only in his native city of Glasgow, but further afield, was born of Scottish parents in the year 1843.

He had a religious upbringing, and at the age of nineteen was called on to address a Gospel meeting. It was during this memorable service

HYMNS AND THEIR WRITERS.   109

that Alexander Stewart realised for the first time in his life, that, while he sought to point others to the Saviour, he himself was a lost sinner. Soon after this, as he lay awake in bed, in sore anxiety of soul, the light of the glorious Gospel shone in, the young man immediately found peace through believing in the finished work of Calvary.

His early life was marked by a fervent zeal for the Master, which found a ready outlet in openair preaching. As years went on, his profession as a lawyer in the city of Glasgow, did not prevent Mr. Stewart from exercising the gift of ministry with which he was endowed, and he rarely had any difficulty in securing and holding an audience. "A man of sterling character," writes a fellowlabourer in the Lord's work, "his rich commanding voice, gentlemanly-bearing, marked ability joined with deep spirituality, secured for him at all times, either outside or inside, a respectful and attentive hearing."

Closely associated with Christians meeting in Union Hall, where for many years he faithfully ministered the Word of Life, Mr. Stewart was a familiar and beloved personality in connection with the various assembly activities in Glasgow. Powerful in the exposition of the Scriptures, he was an acceptable minister on conference platforms throughout the country. Mr. Stewart spent his later years at Prestwick, in Ayrshire, where he was called home on April 27th, 1923.

It is as the writer of "O Lamb of God, we lift our eyes," that the name of Alexander Stewart will always have a place in our hearts, for though he had the pen of a ready writer, and gave to the Church many tuneful lays, yet no other composition of his can surpass this hymn. To fully appreciate the beauty and charm of the sublime lines, is to hear this hymn sung to the grand old Psalm-tune "Martyrdom." This tune, which is used extensively in Scotland, does not, as is generally supposed, go back to the days of the Covenanters, but had its origin towards the end of the eighteenth century. The original form of the melody is in common time. Its first appearance in triple time, to which it is now sung, seems to have been in connection with a collection of sacred musical compositions, sung in St. George's Church, Edinburgh, in 1825.

As the tune became popular, it passed through the hands of a host of revisers, and in consequence had many claimants. Abundant evidence, however, has been produced to show that the composer of "Martyrdom" was Hugh Wilson, a native of Fenwick.

Referring to the time when this tune was first sung in the Scottish Capital, a writer in "The Psalmodist," about eighty years ago, said: "I well remember the day it ("Martyrdom") was first sung in St. George's, Edinburgh, for Dr. Thomson then said to me, 'O man! I could not sing for weeping.'"

Mr. Stewart's only other contribution to Assembly Hymn Books, is also of high merit, and is indeed, a hymn beloved:

> Lord Jesus Christ, we seek Thy face
> Within the veil we bow the knee;
> O let Thy glory fill the place,
> And bless us while we wait on Thee.

The writer strikes his highest note in the closing verse, which ranks with the compositions of some of our foremost hymn writers:

> The brow that once with thorns was bound,
> Thy hands, Thy side, we fain would see;
> Draw near, Lord Jesus, glory-crowned,
> And bless us while we wait on Thee.

JAMES G. SMALL.

IN the year that Alexander Stewart was born, a young Scotsman, who in days to come was to give to the world a hymn that would be blessed to thousands, had reached an eventful stage in his life. For it was this year, after studying under the celebrated Dr. Chalmers, that he was called to the ministry of the Free Church of Scotland. His name was James Grindly Small, and the hymn he wrote is the one beginning:

> I've found a Friend; O, such a Friend!
>   He loved me ere I knew Him;
> He drew me with the cords of love,
>   And thus He bound me to Him.
> And round my heart still closely twine
>   Those ties which nought can sever,
> For I am His, and He is mine,
>   For ever and for ever.

Born in Edinburgh in 1817, Mr. Small was educated at the High School there, from which he proceeded to Edinburgh University. In 1847, Mr. Small became minister of the Free Church at Bervie, near Melrose, A fairly voluminous writer, he produced several poetical works including "Hymns for Youthful Voices," and "Psalms and Sacred Songs." It was in the latter collection, which was published in 1866, that "I've found a Friend" first appeared. Since then, while J. G. Small's other hymns and poems are almost unnoticed, this one is sung with unabated fervour wherever Christ is preached. Mr. Small died at Renfrew, February 11th, 1888.

"I've found a Friend" was an especial favourite with Ira D. Sankey, and he frequently sang it as a solo during the great revival services. To see the beaming face, and to hear the rich baritone voice of the singing evangelist, as he rang out the joyful message, was indeed an inspiration.

On one occasion, when Sankey and Henry Moorhouse were holding meetings at Scarborough, the services were attended by a number of Quaker ladies, among them being a cousin of the Right Honourable John Bright. Wishing to have this hymn sung at one of the meetings, this lady sent a slip of paper to the platform, bearing the following request: "Will Mr. Sankey please repeat the hymn, 'I've found a Friend,' in his usual way?" "In thus wording her note," said Sankey, when telling the story, "she avoided asking me to sing, which is against the custom of the Society of Friends."

How the singing of this hymn wrought a wonderful change in the life of a wayward young man is worthy of recording here. During a cottage meeting held in a lodging-house in the Midlands, a young man, who was an inmate, came into the room where the meeting was held, with the object of bringing ridicule on the little gathering. After the singing of a few hymns, some one engaged in prayer, when the young man rose and asked for the hymn "I've found a Friend." During the singing of the hymn, the youth was seen to be in tears, and before the meeting closed one of the workers had the joy of pointing the wanderer to the Saviour. The next morning he left the town, but before leaving, the young man sent a letter to one of the missioners, in which he wrote: "I asked you to sing that hymn because it was a favourite of my dear sister, who is waiting for me at the gates of heaven. I have now promised to meet her there. By God's help, if we do not meet again on earth, I promise to meet you in heaven. You will always think of me when you

Inset: Dr George Matheson. INNELLAN MANSE. Photo: D. J. Beattie.
The birthplace of "O Love that wilt not let me go."

HYMNS AND THEIR WRITERS.

sing, 'I've found a Friend.' Show this letter to my two other friends."

Thus the singing of this hymn, doubtless recalling memories of happier days, was used of God in bringing a wanderer to the feet of Jesus, and now he was able to sing from the heart:

> I've found a Friend; O, such a Friend!
>   He bled, He died to save me;
> And not alone the gift of life,
>   But His own self He gave me.
> Nought that I have, mine own I'll call,
>   I'll hold it for the Giver;
> My heart, my strength, my life, my all,
>   Are His, and His for ever.

DR. GEORGE MATHESON.

IN the early 'eighties of last century, another Scotsman gave to us a hymn which, though not found in every assembly collection, is frequently used at our meetings.

"O Love, that wilt not let me go," is an exceedingly tender hymn, and was written during a period of extreme mental distress.

George Matheson, the author, was the son of a prosperous Glasgow merchant. From childhood he suffered from impaired eyesight, and by the time the boy had reached the age of eighteen, he was practically blind. This sad handicap does not appear to have discouraged the ambitious youth, and after a successful scholastic career at the university of his native city, Matheson entered the ministry of the Church of Scotland. In 1868, when about twenty-six, he became minister of the Argyllshire parish of Innellan, on the Firth of Clyde.

On a quiet summer evening in the month of June, 1882, Dr. Matheson was seated in his study. He had suffered a severe loss, and as he sat there alone in the darkness greatly distressed, there suddenly flashed upon his mind, the words of the hymn now so well-known. Recalling the wonderful experience through which he passed, the author tells us, that verse by verse seemed to come without effort, as though dictated by someone, the whole of the composition being the work of but a few minutes.

Dr. Matheson was a brilliant scholar and a powerful preacher, and despite the sore affliction of blindness, he rose to considerable eminence in literature. And yet it is doubtful whether any of his literary attainments have reached the high popularity of his famous hymn. He died at North Berwick, in 1906.

Last summer, when on a visit to Innellan, I called at the Manse with a view to obtaining a photograph of the birth-place of "O Love, that wilt not let me go," and as I lingered in the old fashioned study where fifty years before, Dr. Matheson had penned his immortal hymn, there seemed to be wafted to me over the restless waters of the murmuring Clyde, the echo of the opening lines, which, since that memorable day in June, have been sung the world over:

> O Love, that wilt not let me go,
>   I rest my weary soul in Thee;
> I give Thee back the life I owe,
> That in Thine ocean depths its flow
>   May richer, fuller be.

JOSIAH CONDER.

> Thou art the Everlasting Word,
>   The Father's only Son;
> God manifestly seen and heard,
>   And Heaven's beloved One.
> Worthy, O Lamb of God, art Thou,
> That every knee to Thee should bow!

JOSIAH CONDER, the author of this soul-stirring song of praise, once said concerning subjective hymns: "On reading a hymn nobody enquires why it was written or attributes the feelings it depicts to the poet's actual, or, at any rate, present experience." That was a hundred years ago. Times have surely changed, and since then the story of how many an old-fashioned hymn came into being has been told and retold, giving colour and point to the thoughts and feelings which prompted the theme that eventually evolved into sacred verse.

Josiah Conder was the son of a bookseller in Aldersgate, London, where, on September 17th, 1789, the future poet was born. His father and mother were staunch non-conformists, and the boy grew up in the faith of his God-fearing parents. At an early age Josiah lost the sight of his right eye, and fearing the other might be affected, the boy was sent by his parents to be treated by a noted physician. While the patient was undergoing treatment, the physician became the tutor of the studious boy, who thus gained a knowledge of French and Latin, with other studies.

On reaching the age of fifteen, Josiah was taken as assistant into his father's bookshop. Thus coming in contact with people of learning who frequented the shop, the lad soon gave evidence of a pronounced taste for literature, and at the age of twenty-one, we find the youthful aspirant assisting in the production of a volume of poems to which he largely contributed.

It was about this time that Conder began writing hymns, which useful study he did not forsake despite a strenuous literary career, throughout which he was never entirely free from embarrassments of pecuniary struggle. Remembering these conflicting experiences, Conder's hymns, ever hopeful and trustful in spirit, come to the heart of the Christian with especial power and feeling. He was a prolific writer and both his prose and poetical works are numerous.

As a hymn book compiler and editor he was well-known. Amongst his hymnal publications, "The Congregational Hymn Book," issued in 1836, and long recognized as a standard collection of hymns, contained fifty-six of his compositions. Julian, the eminent hymnologist, is high in his praise of Conder, whom he ranks with some of the best writers of the first half of last century. "Conder's hymns," he says, "are the outcome of a deeply spiritual mind. Their variety in metre, in style, and in treatment saves them from the monotonous mannerism which mars the work of many hymn writers. Their theology, though decidedly evangelical, is yet of a broad and liberal kind."

Conder is represented in the "Believers Hymn Book," "Hymns of Light and Love," and "Hymns for Christian Worship," by a single hymn—but one of considerable merit—the opening verse of which has already been given. Here the heart of the poet exults in fullest praise to Christ, the Father's only Son:

> In Thee, most perfectly expressed,
> The Father's glories shine,
> Of the full Deity possessed,
> Eternally Divine!

HYMNS AND THEIR WRITERS.

Many tunes have been adapted to this hymn, but none more suitably express the majesty of the theme than the old melody known as "Arabia."

Josiah Conder died at St. John's Wood, London, on December 27th, 1855.

BERNARD BARTON.

ANOTHER frequently sung hymn in the various Assemblies, written about the same time as "Thou art the Everlasting Word," is the one beginning:

> Walk in the light, so shalt thou know
> That fellowship of love
> His spirit only can bestow,
> Who reigns in light above.

Bernard Barton, commonly known as the "Quaker Poet" is its author. Various hymnal references give Barton's birthplace as Carlisle, where his father, who belonged to a notable Quaker family, was in business as a cotton manufacturer. A letter written by the poet, which recently came under my notice, definitely establishes the fact that his parents removed to London, and the birth of the author of "Walk in the Light" took place on January 31st, 1784, shortly after their arrival at the metropolis.

Bernard was sent to a Quaker school at Ipswich, and on reaching the age of fourteen, became apprenticed to a shopkeeper at Halstead in Essex. After eight years' service he removed to Woodbridge, Suffolk, where he entered into partnership with his brother-in-law, as a coal and corn merchant. Following the death of his young wife, within a year of their marriage, Barton became unsettled, and abandoned business. He proceeded to Liverpool, where he obtained employment as tutor in the family of a city gentleman, but only retained his post for a brief period. Returning to Woodbridge he received a clerkship in a bank. This position Mr. Barton held till his death, which occurred on February 19th, 1849.

The poetical works of Bernard Barton are numerous, and attracted the attention of the English poet Robert Southey, and so opposite a character as Lord Byron. He was for some years in receipt of a state pension of £100, granted to him on the recommendation of Sir Robert Peel. From his works, over twenty hymns have been selected and are at the present time in general use, the best known being "Walk in the Light."

JAMES H. EVANS.

AMONG hymns of praise at the first sound of which the heart of the redeemed so readily responds, there is one commencing:

> As sinners saved we gladly praise
> The Author of redeeming grace;
> Father, 'tis Thine almighty power
> Secures us when the tempests lower.

This excellent hymn, unlike many others not so well matched, has the decided advantage of being set to a bright and appropriate melody, in the grand old Psalm tune "Duke Street."

HYMNS AND THEIR WRITERS.

It is by James Harrington Evans, a hymnist belonging to another school of thought to that of the previous writer; and who died in the same year as Barton. He was the son of Dr. Evans of Salisbury Cathedral, and was born on April 15th, 1785. Educated at Wadham College, Oxford, where he graduated in 1803, Evans entered upon a ministerial career in the Church of England, four years later. At the age of thirty, having previously experienced a great spiritual change, he left the Church of England and became a Baptist minister. He was for many years pastor of John Street Baptist Chapel, Gray's Inn Road, London.

Mr. Evans was the author of several prose works, but is best remembered by the hymns he wrote. In 1818 he compiled "Hymns, Selected chiefly for Public Worship," which contained a number of his own compositions. Besides the hymn already mentioned, possibly his next best known hymn is:

> Faint not, Christian, though the road
> Leading to thy blest abode
> Darksome be, and dangerous too,
> Christ, thy Guide, will bring thee through.

This hymn was written about the year 1833, and has, since then, undergone several changes: the hymn "Fear not, children, though the road," being a transcript, while a further alteration, with the addition of a chorus, provides an arrangement which is popular in America.

James H. Evans removed to Stonehaven, Scotland, where he died on December 1st, 1849.

ERNST C. HOMBURG.

> Jesus, Source of life eternal,
> Jesus! Author of our breath;
> Victor o'er the hosts infernal,
> By defeat, and shame, and death.
> Thou through deepest tribulation
> Deigned to pass for our salvation:
> Thousand, thousand praises be,
> Lord of Glory, unto Thee.

WE are living in a day when the output of new hymns is perhaps greater than at any other period since the days of David the sweet singer of Israel. Many of these song-messages will doubtless live to be sung by generations to come, though by far the greater number will bloom but for a season, only to pass away and be forgotten. "Jesus! Source of life eternal" was written about three hundred years ago, and still finds a place with other hymns of less ripe years. It is a translation from the German by Miss H. K. Burlingham, who is also the writer of many well-known hymns.

Ernst C. Homburg, its author, had a chequered career. Born at the German village of Mihla, in 1605, he early gave promise of a decided gift for literature. At Naumburg in Saxony he became Clerk of the Assizes. Despite this important official appointment, he freely associated with companions of loose habits, and many of his early poems included the debased love and drinking songs characteristic of the times. Regarded by his contemporaries as a poet of the front rank, Homburg won distinction in literature and had almost reached the goal of his ambition when he was stricken with a severe and prolonged illness, which was followed by serious domestic difficulties. In his affliction and distress he cried to God for mercy. That cry was heard, the chains of sin were severed, and his trust was now in the Saviour. From that moment he became a faithful follower of the Lord Jesus, and the pen which up to that time had brought him applause from the secular world, was now used in giving to the Church songs of highest praise, many of which have been translated into English and are in frequent use to-day.

Homburg died at Naumburg in 1681.

JOSEPH SWAIN.

THE early days of Joseph Swain the author of—

> O how the thought that I should know
> Jesus, who suffered here below,

were spent in circumstances somewhat similar to those of the previous writer.

Born at Birmingham in 1761 he was early left an orphan. After serving part of his apprenticeship to the trade of an engraver he removed to London. Here his gift as a lyric-writer and singer led the youth into evil company, where he employed his talent in the writing of songs and plays. In the midst of a reckless life a sudden awakening brought about an intense anxiety of soul, and in his distress, with no one to help him, the youth sought out a bookseller where he might purchase a Bible. It was thus that the wayward young man found the Saviour, and was soundly converted. His new experience now found unrestrained expression in singing the praises of his Saviour, and he very soon directed his poetic gift into a channel of usefulness. The "Walworth Hymns," a collection, the first edition of which was published in 1792, contained nearly 200 of his own compositions, a considerable number of which are still in general use.

In several collections "O how the thought that I shall know" commences with the second verse:

> For ever to behold Him shine!
> For evermore to call Him mine!
> And see Him still before me;
> For ever on His face to gaze,
> And meet His full assembled rays,
> While all His beauty He displays,
> To all His saints in glory.

Another hymn by Swain begins—

> What will it be to dwell above,
> And with the Lord of Glory reign?

Soon after his conversion, while still following his occupation, Joseph Swain turned his attention to the preaching of the Gospel, and when about thirty years of age he was invited to become minister of a Baptist congregation at Walworth, London. Here his faithful preaching of the Word attracted numbers to hear him. In a short time the membership increased from 27 to 200, and the chapel had to be enlarged on three occasions. But his enfeebled constitution could not withstand the arduous strain, and after a comparatively short but successful ministry Joseph Swain died on April 14th, 1796, in his thirty-fifth year.

FREDERICK WHITFIELD.

THERE have been many beautiful hymns written around the ever precious name of Jesus, and while Bernard of Clairvaux's "Jesus! the very thought of Thee," and John Newton's "How sweet the name of Jesus sounds" will always take a foremost place in our affections, there are others whose theme is ever the same. An old favourite is:

> There is a Name I love to hear,
> I love to speak its worth;
> It sounds like music in mine ear—
> The sweetest Name on earth.
>
> Jesus! the name I love so well,
> The name I love to hear;
> No saint on earth its worth can tell,
> No heart conceive how dear.

This hymn was written in 1855 when Frederick Whitfield, its author, was about twenty-six years of age. It was first published in leaflet form and soon afterwards issued in various languages. There is a very pretty story associated with the origin of this hymn, but I have been unable to obtain any proof of its authenticity. It is said that the author was staying with his two sisters, when one morning on coming down to breakfast one sister greeted him with the words, "Oh, Fred, there is a Name I love to hear"; to which he instantly replied, "I love to speak its worth." The other sister at once joined in with, "That sounds like music in mine ear." "Yes," was the brother's ready response, "it is the sweetest name on earth!" Having thus received the first verse by spontaneous conversation, Mr. Whitfield caught the idea and wrote the whole of the hymn.

The "Believers Hymn Book" has chosen a very beautiful and appropriate tune for this hymn.

"Belmont" has been attributed to various composers including Mozart, but it is generally assigned to William Gardiner of Leicester. It appears to be an adaptation from a melody supposed to have been composed by Gardiner and published by him in 1812.

Frederick Whitfield was born at Threapwood, Shropshire, in 1825, and was educated at Trinity College, Dublin. He became a clergyman in the Church of England, and besides being the writer of a number of hymns he is the author of several profitable prose works bearing upon the Scriptures. He died on the 13th September, 1904. His best known hymn is:

> I need Thee, precious Saviour!
>   O Thou art all to me;
> Before the throne for ever
>   I stand complete in Thee.
> Though Satan loud accuses,
>   Yet I can ever see
> The Blood of Christ most precious,
>   The sinner's perfect plea.

ANDREAS BERNSTEIN.

> O, patient, spotless One!
> Our hearts in meekness train
> To bear Thy yoke and learn of Thee,
> That we may rest obtain.

THIS tender little hymn was written more than two hundred years ago by a young German named Christian Andreas Bernstein. He was born at Domnitz, near Halle, where his father was a pastor. After completing his studies at Halle he was ordained as assistant to his father, but three years later, on October 16th, 1699, died at the place of his birth, in his twenty-eighth year.

A few of Bernstein's hymns translated from the German were included in the "Moravian Hymn Book," published in 1754, and have since been copied into various English hymnals.

Very little can be discovered of the life of this youthful hymn writer, but if one may be permitted to judge from the spiritual tone of his poetical outpourings, his must have been a life—at any rate during the period of his hymn writing—spent in close communion with his Saviour. The second verse of the hymn is an example of the writer's fervent adoration, so feelingly expressed—

> Saviour Thou art enough
> The mind and heart to fill;
> Thy life, to calm the anxious soul,
> Thy love, its fear dispel.

And who is there amongst us, who, at some time or other, when the heart, responsive to His tender touch, has not found fullest expression in these lines?

JAMES HUTTON.

ANOTHER composition very similar to the foregoing and a much loved hymn is:

> O teach us more of Thy blest ways,
> Thou holy Lamb of God!
> And fix and root us in Thy grace,
> As those redeemed by blood.

It was written about the year 1742 by James Hutton, a cousin of the celebrated Sir Isaac Newton. He was born in London, in 1715, and on reaching his teens was apprenticed to a bookseller, whom he afterwards succeeded in business.

A few years later, when a wave of spiritual revival swept over Great Britain in consequence of the faithful preaching of the Wesley brothers, the young man was led to the Saviour. Hutton's bookshop now became the rendezvous of many of like mind to himself, and very soon his zeal led him to commence holding meetings in his house, for the preaching of the Gospel.

When Hutton was just twenty-four he became acquainted with Count Zinzendorf (the author of many beautiful hymns in use to-day) who in years to come was to influence, in no small measure, the life of James Hutton. It was when on a visit to Herrnhut, the renowned Moravian settlement, that the two met. The Count was at that time Bishop of the Moravian Church, and Hutton's sympathies having for some time been leaning in that direction, he whole-heartedly threw in his lot with the disciples of Zinzendorf.

Hutton continued to carry on his business as bookseller in London, in which position he lost no opportunity in using a powerful influence towards the development and furtherance of Christian enterprise, both at home and abroad.

In 1741 he printed the second "Moravian Hymn Book." A more comprehensive collection was published thirteen years later, to which Hutton contributed several hymns, and it is from this source that many of his compositions have been taken. The hymns of Hutton follow closely the style of his friend and compeer Zinzendorf. An earnest and devout Christian, he had ever a heart for the Lord's work, and in the prime of life relinquished a prosperous business, that he might entirely devote his time to the cause, particularly interesting himself in missionary work associated with the Moravian movement. These were the days of Whitefield, Cennick, and the Wesleys, and his "Memoir" indicates that he was intimately acquainted with those notable preachers and their work of evangelization.

Hutton died in 1795, in his eightieth year, and was buried at Chelsea.

Amongst his many hymns "O teach us more of Thy blest ways"—originally written "Teach me yet more of Thy blest ways"—is perhaps the sweetest.

GEORGE KEITH.

ANOTHER bookseller, George Keith by name, who flourished in business in London about the same time as Hutton, is credited with the authorship of that stirring hymn:

> How firm a foundation, ye saints of the Lord,
> Is laid for your faith in His excellent word!
> What more can He say, than to you He hath said,
> You who to the Saviour for refuge hath fled?

This hymn, which originally consisted of seven stanzas, first appeared in a collection published by Dr. Rippon in 1787, under the title of "Exceeding great and precious promises," and bearing the single initial "K" as the author's signature. Subsequent editions gave no clue to the authorship, and for some years the verses were ascribed to an unknown person of the name of Keen. The origin of the hymn has been the subject of much enquiry, but now most compilers assign "How firm a foundation" to George Keith. He was the son-in-law of Dr. John Gill, a popular preacher in his day, and as precentor, Keith led the singing in the congregation for many years.

An interesting story relating to this hymn, which is taken from the "Western Sketch-Book," describes a visit to the distinguished American soldier and statesman, General Jackson, and is worthy of recounting here. "The old hero," says the writer, "was then very frail, and had the appearance of extreme old age; but he was reposing with calmness and confidence on the promise and covenant of God." During the conversation which took place, General Jackson turned to his friends and remarked: "There is a beautiful hymn on the subject of the exceeding great and precious promises of God to His people. It was the favourite hymn of my dear wife till the day of her death. It commences with the words: 'How firm a foundation.' I wish you would sing it now." So the little company sang the entire hymn, the old warrior mechanically beating time as it proceeded; then, as the last line of the last verse was reached, his timorous voice rose above the others in evident soul-delight at the reassuring words:

"He'll never—no, never—no, never forsake!"

JOHN BERRIDGE.

Lord Jesus, who did'st once appear
   To grace a marriage feast,
We now beseech Thy presence here,
   To make this wedding blest.

THIS fitting marriage hymn was written by John Berridge, who lived to see more than three-score years and ten, and was himself never married. He was born at Kingston, Nottinghamshire, in 1716. His father was a well-to-do farmer and designed that his son should follow the same calling, but John had neither taste nor inclination for agricultural pursuits.

The first religious impressions of young Berridge were awakened partly through the influence of a school companion and partly through the faithful entreaties of an itinerant tailor who was occasionally employed about the house. Finding his son given much to the study of the Bible, the father decided to give the lad a suitable education that he might go forth to be, as he declared, a "light to the Gentiles."

In 1749 Berridge became curate of Stapleford, near Cambridge, but though he laboured diligently for six years, his ministry was fruitless. His next charge was at Everton, where his early efforts met with the same barren results, till one day the truth of the Gospel was suddenly brought home to his own soul. Thus he was now able to make plain the way of salvation to others, with a power that he had never before experienced. He has left behind an account of the great change which came into his life. "One morning," he says, "I was sitting in my house, and musing upon a text of Scripture, the following words were darted into my mind with wonderful power, and seemed indeed like a voice from heaven, 'Cease from thine own works.' Before I heard these words, my mind was in a very unusual calm; but as soon as I heard them, my soul was in a tempest directly, and tears flowed from my eyes like a torrent. The scales fell from my eyes immediately, and I clearly saw the rock I had been sitting on for nearly thirty years. Do you ask what this rock was? Why, it was some secret reliance on my own works for salvation. I had hoped to be saved, partly in my own name, and partly in Christ's name; though I am told there is salvation in no other name, except in the name of Jesus Christ."

With this new light burning in his soul, John Berridge found his parish too small, and went from county to county proclaiming the Gospel with a zeal which at once provoked the opposition of his bishop, who sharply rebuked him for preaching outside his own parish. But this did not in

HYMNS AND THEIR WRITERS. 131

the least cool the spiritual ardour of this refactory parson, for it is said that he preached often twelve times in one week, journeying many miles over rough country roads in all kinds of weather.

In the midst of his labours he was caught in the great revival current which swept over these islands, consequent upon the work of the Holy Spirit, made manifest through the preaching of Wesley and Whitefield, and he at once associated himself with those zealous evangelists in the work of soul-winning. He was also a close friend of Lady Huntingdon, who was so wonderfully used of God at that time.

But John Berridge was no ordinary man, and though accounted by contemporary writers as eccentric, yet it would have been difficult to find a more earnest and devout soul, who knew both how to attract or enliven the attention of his hearers by characteristic humourous turns of expression, and how to touch their hearts by pathetic allusions or appeals.

It is as a writer of hymns that we remember him specially. The first verse of the marriage hymn here given, has been altered from the original which began: "Since Jesus freely did appear." It was first published in the "Gospel Magazine," in 1775.

His preface to a collection of hymns which he published, is characteristic of the man: "My Saviour and my God, accept this mite of love which is cast into Thy treasury. Give it blessing, and it shall be blessed. What is water in the hymn turn it into wine."

JOHN WITHY.

ANOTHER frequently sung marriage hymn which finds a place in nearly all our Assembly hymn books, begins:

> Lord Jesus, let Thy favour rest
> Upon this bond of love;
> May it be bound in heaven, and blest
> With blessing from above.

John Withy, the author, is also the writer of several devotional hymns, a number of which are to be found in "Hymns for Christian Worship,' as well as in other similar collections. He was born at Downend, Gloucestershire, on October 2nd, 1809. Of a very quiet and retiring disposition, even his own family did not know of some hymns which had been written by him, till after his death.

Mr. Withy was for a long period in fellowship at Bethesda Chapel, Bristol, a place of worship so prominently associated with the early days of Brethren. For many years prior to his home-call —which came in 1882—an affliction, which at intervals caused intense suffering, laid Mr. Withy aside, and it was doubtless during those weary days in the sick chamber that many of his best hymns were composed, including "Where shall the weary turn for rest," which contains these expressive lines:

> Thus, though the cup with anguish fill,
> And nature fail beneath the smart,
> Thou, Lord, hast wondrous love and skill
> To bind and heal the broken heart.

GEORGE BURDER.

> Come ye that know the Saviour's name,
> And raise your thoughts above;
> Let every heart and voice unite
> To sing—that God is love!

THIS hymn was written at Coventry, in 1784, by George Burder, whose name in later years was to become so prominently associated with the founding of such world-wide movements for the furtherance of the Gospel as The Religious Tract, The London Missionary, and The British and Foreign Bible Societies. Born in London, on June 5th, 1752, the boy very early showed some ability in drawing, and he was placed under the tuition of a noted Royal Academy artist. When quite a youth he one day found his way into a chapel, where crowds were flocking to hear George Whitefield preach. So impressed was the young man with what he heard, that he determined to know more about this " new birth," and that night George Burder returned to his home rejoicing in a new-found joy.

At the age of twenty-three he began to preach the Gospel, and having associated himself with the Tabernacle Church in London, he gave up his artistic pursuits for the ministry. In 1778 Burder became pastor of the Congregational Church at Lancaster, and five years later removed to Coventry, where he continued for twenty years. It was here that many of his hymns were written.

Mr. Burder, besides being an acceptable preacher, had a fascile pen, and during the years of his pastorate his writings such as "Village Tracts," and "Sea Sermons" (the latter written for sailors), were widely circulated and greatly used in many remarkable conversions. In his later years, while acting as secretary for the London Missionary Society, Mr. Burder preached at Fetters Lane, where he continued until within a few months of his death, which took place on May 29th, 1832, in his eightieth year.

Besides being the author of a number of hymns, Burder is known to hymnology by his "Collection of Hymns from various Authors," which was published in 1784. This collection is notable because of the fact that it attained to its twenty-fifth edition during the lifetime of the author: an attainment very rarely enjoyed by hymnal compilers. "Come ye that know the Saviour's name," the hymn already quoted, first appeared in this collection along with the author's best known composition which is still used amongst Assemblies, and is to be found in "Hymns of Light and Love" in a slightly altered form:

>Great the joy where Christians meet!
>Christian fellowship how sweet,
>When, our theme of praise the same,
>We exalt Jehovah's name.

JAMES BODEN.

LIVING during the lifetime of Burder was another writer who contributed a few hymns which are to be found in hymnals used by the various assemblies of Brethren. His name was James Boden. He was born on April 13th, 1757, in the house at Chester formerly occupied by Matthew Henry, the well-known commentator. There still lingered about the place many associations of Henry, and it is not improbable that as the boy played in the old summer-house, where, many years previously, the commentator had sought seclusion when engaged upon his notable work, the mind of young Boden would be directed into paths which in days to come ripened into a sincere love for the Word of God; for at the early age of sixteen we find him actively associated with the remnant of the Congregational Church, all that was left of Matthew Henry's once prosperous Presbyterian flock, now driven by stress of circumstances and poverty into a small upper room.

Here the vigorous new life of the young convert very soon manifested itself in a marked degree, and before he had reached his twentieth birthday James Boden was placed in charge of a congregation at Hanley, in the Staffordshire potteries. Keenly interested in young folks he gathered together a number of children for the purpose of instructing them in the Scriptures, which effort developed into a prosperous Sunday School.

In 1796 Mr. Boden became pastor of a chapel in Sheffield, where he continued for more than forty-three years. He died at Chesterfield—two years after retiring from active work—on June

4th, 1841, in his eighty-fifth year. On the last Sunday morning of his stay on earth the sun shone brightly, throwing its rays across his bedchamber. A friend who sat with him remarked on the fact, when the aged saint, his thoughts centred far above, instantly replied:

> He is my Sun, though He forbear to shine,
> I dwell for ever on His heart, for ever He on mine.

Boden wrote several hymns, but only a few are now in general use. In 1801 he assisted Dr. Williams of Sheffield in the compilation of a collection of 600 hymns. To this collection known as "Williams and Boden," can be traced the anonymous modern translation of "Jerusalem my happy home," and it has been suggested that it is not impossible this adaptation may have been by Boden himself.

He is the author of the inspiring hymn:

> Come, all ye saints of God!
> Publish through earth abroad
> Jesus' great fame;
> Tell what His love has done;
> Trust in His name alone;
> Shout to His lofty throne,
> Worthy the Lamb!

WILLIAM REID.

> Mid the splendours of the glory,
>   Which we hope ere long to share,
> Christ, our Head, and we, His members,
>   Shall appear divinely fair;
>   O how glorious!
>   When we meet Him in the air!

BETTER known as editor and compiler of hymns rather than as a hymn writer, William Reid, the author of this hymn, has left behind a few songs of praise which still find a place in several present-day hymnals. Born at Forfar in 1822, he was educated at the Parish School, and for some time served as a pupil teacher. In 1839 Mr. Reid proceeded to King's College, Aberdeen, where he graduated with honours, and after a theological course at Edinburgh he became assistant at Blairgowrie Free Church. Of a keen literary bent, Mr. Reid added to his ministerial activities the duties of editor of Drummond's Stirling Tracts, a position he held for eight years. He afterwards edited "The British Herald," a widely-read religious monthly. Possibly Mr. Reid's best known literary work is "The Blood of Jesus," a useful little book which enjoyed a very extensive circulation.

In 1867 William Reid became minister of Warwick Road Presbyterian Church, Carlisle, which at that time was in a struggling condition. An able exponent of the Word, his powerful preaching and faithful adherence to the fundamentals of the Scriptures very soon attracted numbers from other denominations, and there were many remarkable conversions. While many of the church elders were slow to follow their new minister in his clearly-defined line of apostolic teaching, there were those whose spirituality had been thirsting for "the sincere milk of the Word," and their responsive souls readily drank it in.

Nor were his efforts confined to his own church, for, besides preaching in other places of worship in the neighbourhood where an open door presented itself, Mr. Reid on several occasions drew large numbers to hear him in the old Wesleyan Chapel, where, a century earlier, John Wesley himself had preached.

Towards the close of an eventful eight years' ministry at Carlisle, he seemed to have a premonition from the Lord that "his nets were being disturbed," and realizing that he could no longer continue, he severed his connection with the Presbyterian Church and associated himself with Brethren, whose principles he had in recent years so consistently sought to teach, in face of a prevailing ecclesiastical opposition. By this time, many of Mr. Reid's congregation, enlightened by his teaching, had already left the church and were meeting in a small room in Bank Street. These faithful believers formed the nucleus of Carlisle Assembly, now worshipping in Hebron Hall.

Mr. Reid shortly afterwards removed to Edinburgh where he resided until his home-call, which occurred on August 8th, 1881, in his sixtieth year.

Of a humble and gracious disposition, Mr. Reid ever sought to honour God by his implicit faith, living in sole dependence upon Him, and receiving no fixed stipend from the synod who appointed him. On one occasion, having to make a journey by rail to a distant town, he found himself without the necessary means to take him there. Confident that the Lord would not fail him, Mr. Reid made his way to the station, where a friend, unaware of the pastor's immediate need, handed him the requisite amount of his railway fare. This little

HYMNS AND THEIR WRITERS. 139

incident, related to me by an aged brother who, as a youth, came under the influence of William Reid, appears to have been typical of the man, whose name is still a fragrant memory.

As a hymnal editor Mr. Reid made a notable contribution to the songs of the Church by "The Praise Book," a comprehensive collection of over a thousand hymns, upon the compilation of which he was engaged for about ten years. It was published in 1872, and as its title indicates, contains hymns almost exclusively composed for the praise of God, as distinguished from hymns of human experience. He says in the Preface:—

> "It has been my earnest endeavour, to keep the literature of the work so high, that every composition may be able to bear the criticism of the poet, as well as to meet the varied spiritual necessities of the Christian: for with such a copiousness of the poetic as we find in the Holy Scriptures—with such a subject for praise as 'the Church of God,' 'The Word made flesh' dwelling among us, and having so many beautiful creations of sanctified genius as are now published, a Christian who would serve his generation in the way of producing a book of praise, is under a solemn obligation to present something better than a mere chaos of didactic doggerel."

This collection contains many of the compiler's own compositions.

Besides the hymn "Mid the splendours of the glory," the only other composition by William Reid to be found in Assembly hymn books is the one beginning:

> Ours are peace and joy divine,
>   Who are one with Christ,
> When, like branches in the vine,
>   We abide in Christ.
> As a living grafted shoot,
> Nourished from a hidden root,
> We may bear all holy fruit
>   Through "the love of Christ."

W. P. MACKAY.

> We praise Thee, O God,
> For the Son of Thy love,
> For Jesus who died,
> And is now gone above.
>
> Hallelujah! Thine the glory!
> Hallelujah! Amen!
> Hallelujah! Thine the glory!
> Revive us again!

KNOWN throughout the English-speaking world as the writer of "Grace and Truth," a book of intrinsic worth, which has been used of God in bringing many souls into the Kingdom, Dr. W. P. Mackay is also the author of a number of hymns, his best known being "We praise Thee, O God." How it came into being may not be generally known. During one of his evangelistic missions in the earlier years of his labours, Dr. Mackay was taking part in a prayer meeting, when, with a heart overflowing with love and gratitude to God, he, quite unconscious of poetic effect, gave utterance to the words:

> We praise Thee, O God,
> For the Son of Thy love,
> For Jesus who died,
> And is now gone above.

He afterwards adopted them as the first verse of this hymn of praise now so well known.

William Paton Mackay was born at Montrose on May 13th, 1839. Intended for the medical profession he was educated at Edinburgh University, but while yet a student and not long converted, he gave unmistakable evidence that his thoughts and desires lay in another direction. These were the days when the saintly Duncan Matheson was being so mightily used in the

HYMNS AND THEIR WRITERS. 141

Gospel, and one day hearing that the Scottish evangelist was preaching to the crowds at a fair some miles distant, young Mackay determined to go and join him. In this way, while passing through college he devoted the greater part of his spare time in preaching the good news of salvation. Thus began a work for God, the fruits of which heaven alone will reveal in a coming day.

When about thirty years of age Mr. Mackay gave up the practice of medicine, just when he had obtained his M.D. diploma, and accepted an invitation to the pastorate of a Presbyterian Church at Hull, where he continued till his home-call, which came on August 22nd, 1885.

Dr. Mackay was a man of pronounced individuality and character, revealing a remarkable energy and capacity for work. As as instance of his strenuous labours he is said to have travelled 6000 miles by rail, during the first six months of 1875, preaching the Gospel in various parts of the British Isles, often returning to his home about midnight, so that he might be back to his beloved flock on Lord's Day. On the occasion of the first visit of Moody and Sankey to this country in 1873-74, he took an active part in the great mission, this being work in which the heart of Dr. Mackay delighted. As an exponent of the Scriptures his help was much sought after: "men eminent in Christian work—Mr. D. L. Moody with others—have acknowledged their obligations to Dr. Mackay as a teacher of the English Bible, and have preached the Word with greater fulness and certainty for having been closeted with him over the pages which present it to people's view."

Nearly the whole period of his pastorate at Hull —his first and only one—he took no fixed income, looking alone to the Lord to supply his needs;

and these were abundantly supplied through a box placed in the lobby of the church. In this he showed a self-denying spirit, guided in no small measure by a desire that his congregation might be better able to devote more fully to the Lord's work in other spheres of labour.

A charming pen-picture of this wonderful man of God is given by one of his biographers. Thus he writes:—

> "His style of exposition and address was unique, and his matter bristled with illustration and anecdote, drawn from his long and varied experience and capacious memory. He was often abrupt, sometimes startling his hearers by the oddity of his expressions, and frequently humourous. His fervid, rugged eloquence at all times compelled the attention of his audience, whether he was speaking from the platform or the pulpit, and his congregation never left without having learned some fresh truth or gained further insight into an old one."

Dr. Mackay wrote a number of hymns, but few of them have achieved prominence on the ground of literary merit; and yet God has wonderfully used these songs of praise in their own particular sphere. Of his compositions, seventeen are to be found in William Reid's "Praise Book," published in 1872. Besides the hymn already referred to, two others by Dr. Mackay, are equally familiar—"Worthy, worthy is the Lamb," and:

> The Lord is risen: now death's dark judgment flood
> Is passed in Him who bought us by His blood.

He is also the author of the Gospel hymn:

> "Look unto Me, and be ye saved!"
> Look, men of nations all;
> Look, rich and poor; look, old and young;
> Look, sinners, great and small.

When on holiday at Portree, Dr. Mackay met with a serious accident as he was going on board the steamer which was to take him back to Oban,

ALEXANDER STEWART.

DOUGLAS RUSSELL.

where he had been staying. He was carried ashore where medical aid was immediately obtained, but on the day following Dr. Mackay passed away, one of his last utterances being, "For Thine own glory." He was in his forty-seventh year.

DOUGLAS RUSSELL.

Worthy, worthy, worthy, Thou of adoration—
 Glory in the highest! glad praise we offer Thee;
Crowned with glory, honour—worthy coronation!
 Thee on the throne, O Son of God, we see!

THE sound of this soul-inspiring hymn of worship, which, again and again has moved thousands of God's children, recalls a happy afternoon spent in company with its genial author, Mr. Douglas Russell of Weston-super-Mare. Mr. Russell, who was then in his ninetieth year was one of the last living links of the great Moody and Sankey movement which stirred Great Britain from end to end, toward the close of last century.

Born at Old Cumnock, Ayrshire, he was converted when a youth of nineteen, at a time of general awakening in Scotland. He received his first spiritual impression through the ministry of Mr. E. P. Hammond, the American evangelist and author of "I feel like singing all the time." Mr. Russell soon afterwards devoted himself to the Lord's work, and travelled extensively, preaching and singing the Gospel. During his long and varied experience he came in contact with most of the well-known preachers of his time, and assisted Sankey in leading the singing on several occasions.

It was my privilege to hear from the lips of the veteran evangelist and hymn writer, the story of how the steps of D. L. Moody, that plain-looking American preacher, were directed to these shores of ours, and of his memorable visit a year later. And as we sat together in the sunshine of a beautiful summer day, I seemed to be transported to days and scenes which will ever be memorable.

It is not generally known that Mr. Russell was mainly instrumental in directing Mr. Moody's thoughts to evangelistic work in England. It was during his second visit to America in 1870-72, when Mr. Russell was conducting a Gospel mission in New York, that the two evangelists met. At the close of the mission, Moody said in his usual blunt way: "I want you to come to Chicago"; to which Mr. Russell replied, "I'll go to Chicago if the way is clear, on condition that you go back with me to England in the summer." The outcome was that the two evangelists embarked for England on May 24th, 1872.

They were much together, and during his visit to this country, God used Moody to such an extent, that it was decided that, should the Lord open up the way, he would return to Great Britain the following summer. Mr. Moody accompanied Mr. Russell to Dublin where Mr. Henry Varley, a noted preacher, was delivering a series of addresses to Christians. In the course of his remarks, at one of these meetings, the speaker said, "The world has yet to see what God can do with a man who is fully consecrated." Moody then and there asked God that he might be that man—a prayer which was answered in a remarkable way.

It will be remembered that D. L. Moody came back to this country in June 1873, bringing with him one who was to be his partner in the Gospel for nearly thirty years—Ira D. Sankey.

The American evangelists were met at Liverpool by Douglas Russell, Harry Moorhouse and John Houghton. They repaired to a private room in the Great Western Hotel, where the little party spent a time waiting on God in prayer. Thus, at the throne of grace, began a work which God wonderfully honoured in the salvation of countless precious souls.

As I listened to the recital of a story which was destined to become historic, I could not but observe how the eyes of the veteran evangelist lit up at the remembrance of those bygone days. The story he told was indeed characteristic of Moody. Mr. George Bennett, of York, having read of the American evangelist's previous visit, had written to Moody in March asking him if he should ever come back to England, would he kindly remember York. Moody replied by the first mail, fixing Sunday, June 21st, for commencing work in York. "How like the man!" was my friend's pertinent comment. And as Mr. Russell told the story, he smiled with evident pleasure at the recollection of his big-hearted and enthusiastic friend. From the other side of the Atlantic, 4000 miles away, fully three months before, he fixed the engagement, and came to fulfil it without further notice!

At the close of the little prayer meeting in the hotel, Mr. Moody caused a telegram to be sent to Mr. Bennett, announcing his arrival in England, and asking if he was ready. "Poor Bennett!"

said Mr. Russell, "he had been patiently waiting for a confirmatory letter nearer the time; so he replied to Moody that he would be better prepared next week." This was not encouraging; nevertheless the evangelists arranged to go to York on the following Saturday evening. On their arrival, almost every door was closed to the Americans, who were viewed with prejudice and suspicion. At last the Wesleyans agreed to open their chapel, and here the visitors preached and sang for five weeks. From York they went to Sunderland, and the largest hall that town could afford was crowded from the start.

How God blessed the efforts of those faithful servants in the days that followed, is known to most; the fruits of which will only be revealed through the riches of grace, in a day to come.

Years after, Mr. Russell sat by Sankey's bedside. Moody had long since gone to his reward. "It is May 17th, 1908," said Mr. Russell, with a note of pathos in his voice as he recalled the memorable scene. "Mr. Sankey is sadly worn and blind now; he admits that his singing days are over, and that only a few months could elapse before he too would be 'Out of the shadowland into the sunshine.' I sing him one of my songs, the chorus of which goes:

> I'm trusting, I'm trusting,
> I rest in Thee alone;
> Thy name and blood my only plea
> Before the throne.

This was possibly the last song he would hear on earth. As we parted, he said, 'Tell the friends in England that "On Christ the solid rock I stand,"' (adding in an undertone 'There's no other rock!') 'and I am just waiting at the threshold until the Master calls me in.'" That call came on August 14th, 1908, when he went in to take his part in the singing of the New Song.

Mr. Russell is the author of a considerable number of hymns in use to-day, many of which may be found in "Hymns of Light and Love." It is a remarkable circumstance that the poetic muse did not stir within him till well past middle life, his first hymn, "Love, deep and strong," having been written on his fifty-first birthday. He was actively associated with the Assembly at Weston-super-Mare, and notwithstanding his advanced age he attended the meetings with regularity, frequently walking the distance of nearly two miles each way.

Up to within a short time of his home-call—which came on November 14th, 1933, in his ninety-second year—Douglas Russell, though, of course, past active service, still retained much of his youthful charm and zeal for the spreading of the "Good News" in song and story.

P. P. BLISS.

"Man of Sorrows!" what a name
For the Son of God, who came
Ruined sinners to reclaim!
Hallelujah! what a Saviour!

WHEN Moody and Sankey were in Paris, holding meetings in the old church, which, earlier in the century, Napoleon had placed at the disposal of Evangelicals, Mr. Sankey frequently sang this hymn as a solo, asking his French congregation to join in the single phrase, "Hallelujah! what a Saviour!" which they did with remarkable enthusiasm. Singular though it may seem, the word "Hallelujah" is the same in almost every language, the world over.

This hymn was written by P. P. Bliss, in 1876, at a Gospel meeting in Farwell Hall, Chicago, conducted by Henry Moorhouse, the noted evangelist. Amongst early writers in Sankey's "Sacred Songs and Solos," Bliss takes a prominent place. He was both poet and musician, and practically all his hymns were set to music by himself. These very quickly came into public favour, and the advent of the great Moody and Sankey mission of half-a-century ago, which, in its course, carried the sweet songs from continent to continent, at once established them in heart and home. He is the author of "Whosoever will," "Free from the law," "Almost persuaded," "Hold the fort," "I am so glad that Jesus loves me," and a great number of popular Gospel songs, which, even in these days of many new hymns, have lost none of their old-time power and sweetness.

When he was thirty years old, an event occurred which Mr. Bliss regarded as one of the most important in his life; this was his meeting with D.

MY REDEEMER

P. P. BLISS   JAMES McGRANAHAN

P. P. BLISS.

"My Redeemer" was the last hymn he wrote,

L. Moody, who was at that time holding Gospel services in Chicago. Being possessed with a sweet, sympathetic bass voice of splendid tone and quality, Mr. Bliss's powerful singing at once attracted the attention of the evangelist. This memorable meeting had far-reaching results. The vivid impression of the unmistakable power of Gospel song which Mr. Moody received when he met Mr. Bliss, forms an epoch in a movement that has been among the most blessed and remarkable during the last half century.

Mr. Bliss was a fairly prolific writer. To him hymn-writing was a spontaneous out-flow of the emotion and melody with which his soul was filled. His hymns breathe the spirit of devotion. With him the "Coming of the Lord" was indeed a Scripture truth, so real and vivid that his life felt the inspiration of it in everything he said or did. This is exemplified in the last verse of "Man of Sorrows," where the writer strikes a note of exultation in the words:

> When He comes, our glorious King,
> All His ransomed home to bring,
> Then anew this song we'll sing:
>   Hallelujah! what a Saviour!

Often he would come to his wife with the theme of a hymn, with his face shining and his eyes moist with tears, and would ask for prayers that God would bless the hymn. At other times, when he found that God was using his songs to bring out some precious truth of the Gospel, or the exaltation of the Lord Jesus, his heart would overflow with joy.

Of this singing evangelist, D. L. Moody wrote: "As a writer and singer of Gospel songs he was, in my estimate, the most highly honoured of God of any man of his time; and with all his gifts, he was the most humble man I ever knew."

Among the numerous hymns by which this sweet singer will ever be remembered, mention should be made of the one beginning:

> I will sing of my Redeemer,
> And His wondrous love to me:
> On the cruel cross He suffered,
> From the curse to set me free.

This was his last composition.

There is a pathetic interest attached to this hymn, it being Mr. Bliss's last composition, having been written a few days before his tragic death. The manuscript was discovered by Mr. James McGranahan amongst his friend's belongings, and he wrote for it the beautiful tune to which it has since been sung.

Philip Paul Bliss was called home on December 29th, 1876. With his wife he was travelling toward Chicago, when at Ashtabula, Ohio, a railway bridge collapsed and the train was thrown into the stream below. Mr. Bliss might have escaped, but in an endeavour to rescue his wife from the burning carriage, he lost his life. He was then thirty-eight years of age.

H. G. SPAFFORD.

ANOTHER hymn which is still a general favourite is:

> When peace, like a river, attendeth my way,
> When sorrows, like sea billows, roll;
> Whatever my lot, Thou hast taught me to say,
> "It is well, it is well with my soul!"

This hymn was written in the same year as "Man of Sorrows," and was sung for the first time at a meeting in Farwell Hall, Chicago, by Mr. P. P. Bliss, who composed the tune. The writer of the words was Mr. H. G. Spafford.

How the hymn came to be written is a touching story. In 1874, when the French steamer "Ville de Havre" was crossing the Atlantic on its return journey from America, it met with disaster. On Board the steamer was a Mrs. Spafford with her four children. In mid-ocean the steamer came in collision with a large sailing vessel. In half-an-hour the "Ville de Havre" sank and nearly all on board perished. When the collision took place, the distracted mother got her children out of their berths and up on deck. Realising that in a few moments the vessel would go down, Mrs. Spafford knelt with her children, asking God that they might be saved; or be made willing to die if it was His will. When the vessel sank the children were lost. The mother was picked up among some floating wreckage, and some days later she was landed at Cardiff. From that port Mrs. Spafford cabled to her husband, a lawyer in Chicago, the message, "Saved alone." Mr. Spafford started immediately for England to bring his wife to Chicago. Mr. Moody, who at that time was holding Gospel meetings at Edinburgh, made a journey to Liverpool to try to comfort the bereaved parents, and was greatly cheered to find that they were able to say: "It is well; the will of God be done." A comforting fact in connection with the sad event was that in one of the meetings conducted by Moody and Sankey in Chicago, a short time prior to their sailing for Europe, the children had been converted to God.

Two years later, when Sankey was staying at the home of Mr. and Mrs. Spafford, during a series of Gospel meetings in Chicago, Mr. Spafford wrote the hymn, "It is well with my soul," in commemoration of the death of his children.

A business man who had suffered some heavy reverses during a financial crisis, and was in deep despondency, on hearing the story of the hymn, exclaimed: "If Spafford could write such a beautiful resignation hymn, I will never complain again.

Though it is probable the name of Mr. Spafford might never have been known beyond the circle of his professional calling as a Chicago lawyer, but for his hymn "It is well with my soul," he was, nevertheless, a faithful and zealous worker for the Master. A diligent student of God's Word, Mr. Spafford became so profoundly interested in the Second Coming of Christ, that he and his wife decided to go to Jerusalem, and there await the coming of the Lord. In the last verse of the hymn, the writer gives unbounded expression of the aspiration and longing of his heart in the words:

> But, Lord, 'tis for Thee, for Thy coming, we wait;
> The sky, not the grave, is our goal;
> O trump of the angel! O voice of the Lord!
> Blessed hope! blessed rest of my soul!

W. D. WHITTLE.

Our Lord is now rejected,
   And by the world disowned,
By the many still neglected,
   And by the few enthroned;
But soon He'll come in glory!
   The hour is drawing nigh,
For the crowning day is coming
   By and by.

MAJOR WHITTLE, the author of this stirring hymn, ranks among the most successful writers of hymns used in the Evangelistic movements of the last two generations. He was born at Chicopee Falls, Massachusetts, November 22nd, 1840. At the outbreak of the American Civil War, in 1861, he enlisted in the 72nd Illinois Infantry, and was severely wounded at the battle of Vicksburg, which resulted in the loss of an arm.

It was while he lay in hospital, far from home and friends, that young Whittle recalled the fact that his mother, on the morning of his departure for the war, had given him a New Testament, which, till that moment had remained at the bottom of his soldier's haversack, unopened. He took up the precious Book, and as the young man read page after page, he realised as he had never done before, that he was a lost sinner, and dropping on his knees he cried to God for mercy. Thus, in the quiet of that hospital ward, Daniel Webster Whittle passed from death unto life, by trusting in the atoning blood of the Saviour of the world.

Shortly after the war closed, Major Whittle happened to meet D. L. Moody, and it was due to the influence of the great evangelist, and in obedience to the call from the Lord, that Major

Whittle, some years later, gave up his position in business to devote his life to evangelistic work.

His name is a familiar one in the history of the great Moody and Sankey missions to Great Britain. At the close of Mr. Moody's mission in Dublin in the early nineties, Major Whittle and Mr. George C. Stebbins continued the campaign in some of the smaller towns of Ireland, with a view to reaching the people of outlying districts, who were cut off from the privileges the people of the cities enjoyed. There was a deep interest everywhere manifested, and though the mission was void of anything of a spectacular nature, it was evident by the eagerness with which the warm-hearted Irish folks listened to the simple Gospel story, that a work of grace was being wrought in their midst.

Mr. Stebbins, who is now in his eighty-ninth year, is one of the last of the sweet singers of the days of Sankey. He is the composer of the music of a large number of the best known Evangelistic hymns, including Fanny Crosby's "Some day the silver cord will break."

The last meetings of that memorable winter were held in Belfast, where the various places of worship united, and a widespread spirit of enquiry was awakened among the people, when many were lead to the Saviour.

Major Whittle's last mission to Great Britain, when he was again accompanied by Mr. Stebbins, was during the winter of 1896-97, spent in Scotland. The cities visited were Edinburgh, Glasgow, Aberdeen, Inverness, as well as several smaller towns.

The Major loved children, and had a happy faculty of presenting the truths of the Gospel in such a way as to make it attractive and easily

HYMNS AND THEIR WRITERS.

understood by the young folks. Wherever he was conducting meetings he invariably held special services for children, and in order to create interest he gave blackboard illustrations and chemical experiments, to make the truths plain.

The greater part of Major Whittle's Evangelistic work was spent in conjunction with Mr. James McGranahan.

He began writing hymns in 1877, using the pen-name of "El Nathan." Characterised by faithfulness to Scriptural teaching, his hymns soon became recognised as among the best in use in those stirring times, and were in favour almost everywhere, even as they are to-day.

Besides "The crowning day is coming," other familiar hymns by Major Whittle include: "There shall be showers of blessing," "I know whom I have believed," "Jesus is coming," "I looked to Jesus," "Come believing," and that joyous song of the redeemed:

> Come sing, my soul, and praise the Lord,
> Who hath redeemed thee by His blood;
> Delivered thee from chains that bound,
> And brought thee to redemption ground.

Major Whittle passed away at Northfield, March 4th, 1901.

JAMES McGRANAHAN.

REFERENCE has already been made to James McGranahan, whose work as author and composer of this particular type of hymn is well known. The "Believers Hymn Book" and "Hymns of Light and Love" contain only one of his compositions:

> Oh, what a Saviour—that He died for me!
> From condemnation He hath set me free;
> "He that believeth on the Son," saith He,
>   "Hath everlasting life."

Mr. Stebbins, in his "Memoirs and Reminiscences," tells of the first meeting—dramatic in its setting—of Mr. McGranahan and Major Whittle, men who were destined to become known and loved on two continents. They had each gone to Ashtabula in search of information relating to their mutual friends, Mr. and Mrs. P. P. Bliss, who had lost their lives in the great railway disaster. Moving about in the crowd which had gathered, Mr. McGranahan recognised the Major, although they had never met before. Stepping up to him, he said, "Mr. Bliss was one of my dearest friends; my name is McGranahan."

Mr. Bliss had frequently spoken to Major Whittle of McGranahan as being a man who should devote his talent to the Lord's work. "These facts," writes Mr. Stebbins, when telling the story, "flashed to mind as the salutation was given, and he said to himself: 'Here stands the very man that is needed to take Mr. Bliss's place.'" He invited Mr. McGranahan to visit him in Chicago, where he was conducting the meetings inaugurated by Moody and Sankey—they having gone on to their next campaign. "Mr. McGranahan accepted the invitation," continues Mr. Stebbins, "and I well remember his coming and the pleasure it gave me to meet him. I was there assisting the Major in the meetings referred to."

Entering at that time upon this phase of his career was timely, for he came well equipped as a leader, and as a singer and writer of Gospel songs, in all of which Mr. McGranahan proved to be an outstanding figure in the ranks of Evangelists of those days.

It was at this time, while at Chicago, that Mr. McGranahan wrote the music of "I will sing of my Redeemer"—P. P. Bliss's last hymn—the words of which were found in Mr. Bliss's trunk that escaped destruction at Ashtabula. It was in this way that Mr. McGranahan began hymn-writing, and his compositions soon came into popular favour wherever they were sung. His compositions are marked by their originality as expressed in his attractive melodies, combined with musical skill in the treatment of his themes, and the adaptation of his music to the truth to be sung.

Among the many hymns set to music by Mr. McGranahan, which, after the passing of well-nigh fifty years have lost none of their popularity and power, may be mentioned: "There shall be showers of blessing," "The crowning day is coming," "Behold what manner of love," and "Are you coming home to-night."

"In his career as an Evangelist," says Mr. Stebbins, "he impressed those who came under his influence as being a man not only endowed with rare gifts, but one singularly pure in character, with a simple, unwavering faith in his Lord and the work committed to him."

After many years of constant labour in the

Evangelistic field, failing health compelled him to retire to private life; but his remaining years, even to the last, were spent in writing hymns for use in the Master's service.

James McGranahan died at his home in Ohio on July 9th, 1907, at the age of sixty-seven, resting upon his favourite verse—John 6. 47, the text from which he wrote the hymn already quoted. The chorus contains the essence of the Gospel, and has a sweet familiarity:

> "Verily, verily," I say unto you:
> "Verily, verily," message ever new!
> "He that believeth on the Son"—'tis true!
> **"Hath** everlasting life."

H. GRATTAN GUINNESS.

> Crowned with thorns upon the tree,
> Silent in Thine agony;
> Dying, crushed beneath the load
> Of the wrath and curse of God.

TO have penned these sublime lines, the writer must surely have spent many hallowed moments "dwelling on Mount Calvary"; for, as the hymn proceeds, the heart of the singer instinctively responds to the song, and all unconsciously one is drawn to the foot of the Cross, there to view anew that sacred scene which is ever precious to the child of God.

Its author is Dr. H. Grattan Guinness. Of Irish parentage, he was born at Mountpellier, near Dublin, on August 11th, 1835, and received his education at Cleveland and Exeter. His

DR. H. GRATTAN GUINNESS.

J. DENHAM SMITH.

father was a captain in the Indian army, and died when the boy was only fourteen years old. Falling into evil company, Henry left home two years later and sailed for Mexico as a midshipman. On his return from this voyage, his younger brother Robert, with whom he shared a bedroom, told him of his conversion. So full of his new-found joy was the lad that he could talk of nothing else, and it was far into the night before the two brothers fell asleep. Through it all Henry had been silent and thoughtful, and next morning came down to the family circle a changed young man.

Soon after, with a view to taking up farming, he crossed to Ireland, and for a while settled down in Tipperary. Here he became engrossed with the pleasures of an outdoor life, until a seemingly trivial incident recalled him to thought which led to his establishment on the Rock of Ages, and his entire consecration to God.

Before he was twenty-one Mr. Guinness had been marvellously used in winning souls, and pursued open-air preaching, fired with the zeal inborn of the Holy Spirit. Older men sought to damp the ardour of the youth, but such opposition to what he felt was the will of the Lord only increased his fervour. His mother's house was crowded with enquirers, sometimes as many as seventy in one day; and at Cheltenham, services which he commenced on the Promenade were, after a time, held in the Town Hall. Wonderful meetings soon afterwards followed in Wales and Scotland. Later he was invited to the United States of America, where he was greatly used in the Revival of 1858-59, and when the same wave of spiritual blessing swept over this country he laboured unceasingly in proclaiming the Gospel.

He was married in 1860 to Miss Fanny Fitzgerald, who afterwards took so full a part in the work to which God had called him, including the founding of Harley College for Missionary students, and the forming of the Regions Beyond Missionary Union, to work in Congo, India and Peru.

In this connection the first attempt to commence the training of young men with a view to missionary work took place in a house in Dublin, in 1865, when Mr. Guinness conducted a theological class. To this class came Hudson Taylor, and several other of its members became missionaries in China. Young Barnardo was also a regular attender of the class at one time.

Itinerant evangelical work was continued for some years after this, and pioneer work in France occupied some time, but in 1873 the East London Institute was founded, and then began those labours for the work of God overseas by which Dr. Grattan Guinness is most remembered. Dr. and Mrs. Guinness lived on "faith lines," and conducting their work on these principles, God signally honoured their labours so that men were enabled to go forth to all parts of the world.

The Congo Balolo Mission was started as a result of the need of Central Africa made known through the journeys of Dr. Livingstone and H. M. Stanley.

Dr. Guinness was a remarkable personality, and in his self-imposed task of promoting interest in foreign missions, he toured the country delivering lantern addresses. I remember when, as a boy, being taken by my mother to one of his missionary meetings in the south of Scotland, and have still a vivid recollection of the impression upon my young mind at that time, when the hymn "From Greenland's icy mountains" was thrown on the screen, line after line being beautifully illustrated, each changing picture appearing to dissolve simultaneously as the hymn proceeded.

Dr. Guinness wrote several books, his work on "The Historical interpretation of Prophesy in relation to the Second Advent" being his best known literary effort. It is, however, as a writer of hymns that brings his name under review in the present instance. He is the author of numerous hymns—many of which were printed privately to enclose in letters and parcels, and for general distribution. Of these, the following were included in "The Enlarged London Hymn Book," published in 1873: "How beautiful the Saviour's feet," "Yes, Thou art mine, my blessed Lord," and "Thou art my joy, Lord Jesus."

"Crowned with thorns upon the Tree," usually sung to the plaintive melody "Dunstan," is considered to be one of his sweetest compositions. In this hymn the soul of the singer at once experiences a peculiar calm and restfulness as the heart breathes out the language of a soul at peace with God, so touchingly expressed in these verses:

> On Thy pierced and bleeding breast
> Thou dost bid the weary rest;
> Rest there from the world's false ways,
> Rest there from its vanities.
>
> Rest in pardon and relief,
> From the load of guilt and grief;
> Rest in Thy redeeming blood,
> Rest in perfect peace with God.

On June 21st, 1910, when in his seventy-sixth year, Dr. H. Grattan Guinness was called home to be for ever with the Lord.

EDWARD MOTE.

My hope is built on nothing less
Than Jesus' blood and righteousness;
I dare not trust the sweetest frame,
But wholly lean on Jesus' name.
　　On Christ the solid Rock I stand;
　　All other ground is sinking sand.

NEARLY a hundred years ago, a workman was making his way along Holborn Hill, London. He had recently found peace for his troubled soul, after years of waywardness and careless living, and as he walked to his work in the early hours of that quiet morning, before the great city was yet astir, he began to meditate on the riches of redeeming grace, which had obtained for him eternal security in Christ Jesus. Such peace of mind he had never before experienced, and in the ecstacy of his new found joy, involuntarily there came to him the words:

　　"On Christ the solid Rock I stand,
　　All other ground is sinking sand."

Jotting down the two lines on a scrap of paper, he felt that the message was God-given. All that day as he toiled at his carpenter's bench, the one theme of assurance and security in his Saviour seemed to be uppermost in his mind. That night before retiring to rest, he committed to paper the greater part of the hymn we now know so well; the remaining lines being completed the following day.

The name of the writer is Edward Mote. Soon after his conversion, Mr. Mote, while still following his occupation as carpenter, turned his attention to the Lord's work, and some years later became pastor of a Baptist Church at Horsham,

EDWARD MOTE.

HYMNS AND THEIR WRITERS.

Sussex, where he continued to minister for more than twenty years.

In November, 1874, when Mr. Mote was in his seventy-eighth year, his health began to decline, but as the strength of the aged saint failed, his unbounded confidence in God seemed to be renewed. "I think I am going to heaven," he said; "yes, I am nearing port. The truths I have preached I am now living upon, and they will do to die upon. Ah! the precious blood! The precious blood which takes away all our sins; it is this which makes peace with God." And thus in quiet confidence he passed away, trusting only in the merit of the precious blood of which he sang.

Near the pulpit, in the church at Horsham where he ministered, is a tablet to the memory of Mr. Mote, which bears this testimony:

> In loving memory
> of
> MR. EDWARD MOTE,
> who fell asleep in Jesus November 13th, 1874,
> aged 77 years.
>
> "For 26 years the beloved Pastor of this church, preaching Christ and Him crucified, as all the sinner can need, and all the saint can desire."

W. O. CUSHING.

IT is interesting to note that since the day, now far distant, when Augustus Toplady gave to the world his immortal hymn, "Rock of Ages," many subsequent writers have used the scriptural simile, based no doubt on the text, "My strong Rock, for a house of defence."—Psalm 31. 2.

Another hymn of like character to be found in assembly hymn books which, since it was written, has been a comfort and solace to many a weary one in times of trial, when the day seemed dark and the way long, is the one beginning:

> Oh, safe to the Rock that is higher than I,
> My soul in its conflicts and sorrows would fly;
> So sinful, so weary, Thine, Thine would I be;
> Thou blest "Rock of Ages," I'm hiding in Thee.

It was written at Moravia, New York, in 1876, by William O. Cushing. The author has recorded that "Hiding in Thee" was the outcome of many tears, many heart-conflicts and soul-yearnings, of which the world can know nothing. The occasion of its birth was during the world-wide Moody and Sankey mission. Mr. Cushing, whose hymns had already gained considerable reputation, received a note from Sankey asking him to send something new to help him in his Gospel work. "A call from such a source, and for such a purpose," says Mr. Cushing, "seemed a call from God. I so regarded it and prayed: 'Lord give me something that will glorify Thee.' It was while thus waiting that 'Hiding in Thee' pressed to make itself known."

On receiving the manuscript from his friend, Sankey at once perceived the usefulness of the hymn, and wrote the sweet and appropriate tune, to which it has since been sung: a composition which, in no small measure, has contributed to the general favour bestowed upon the hymn.

William O. Cushing was born at Hingham, Massachusetts, U.S.A., on December 31st, 1823, and is the author of several well-known hymns, including: "Jesus knows thy sorrow," "Follow on!" "Ring the bells of Heaven," and that delightful children's hymn:

> When He cometh, when He cometh,
> To make up His jewels,
> All His jewels, precious jewels,
> His loved and His own.

E. P. STITES.

IN the same year that "Hiding in Thee" was written, Moody was in Chicago, when a newspaper cutting bearing some printed verses, was handed to him. After reading the verses through, he passed the cutting to his friend Sankey, asking him to write a tune for the words. He did so, and thus began the mission of that beautiful hymn:

> Simply trusting every day,
> Trusting through a stormy way;
> Even when my faith is small,
> Trusting Jesus, that is all.

Edgar Page Stites, the writer of this hymn, was a prominent business man in Cape May, New Jersey. He is the author of a number of hymns, including the old favourite, "Beulah Land." In the course of some correspondence about twenty years ago, Mr. Stites sent me the following verse in his own handwriting taken from his popular hymn:

> The Saviour comes and walks with me,
> And sweet communion here have we;
> He gently leads me with His hand,
> For this is heaven's borderland.

He was then in his seventy-seventh year, over six feet tall, and remarkable, too, was the fact that the eyes with which he "Looked away across the sea," had never required glasses.

Referring to the former hymn, there is a touching story. A Christian worker visited a woman who was suffering from an incurable disease; but great as was her bodily pain, her distress of mind seemed to be greater still. "Can't you trust yourself in God's hand?" asked her friend. "No," came the sad reply, "I can't leave myself there." After reading to her a portion of God's Word, the Christian friend sang the hymn, "Simply trusting," and as he sang there appeared to come over the sufferer a wonderful change. "Ah," she said, "I can trust Him this moment; is it like that?" And together they sang:

> Trusting as the moments fly,
> Trusting as the days go by;
> Trusting Him whate'er befall,
> Trusting Jesus, that is all.

The poor sufferer never lost her trust in Jesus, and when a few months later, she entered the land where there is no more pain, it was with the words on her lips:

> "Trusting Jesus, that is all."

J. H. GILMORE.

He leadeth me, oh! blessed thought,
Oh! words with heavenly comfort fraught,
Whate'er I do, where'er I be,
Still 'tis God's hand that leadeth me!

JOSEPH HENRY GILMORE, the writer of this hymn, was born at Boston, on April 29th, 1834. He became Professor of Hebrew at Newton Theological Institute, and for some time held a Baptist Ministerial charge at Fisherville, Newhampshire, and at Rochester, New York.

"He leadeth me" was written in 1862, at the close of a service which the author had conducted in the First Baptist Church of Philadelphia. Mr. Gilmore had taken as his theme, the 23rd Psalm, specially emphasising the blessedness of being led by God—of the mere fact of His leadership—altogether apart from the way in which He leads us, and what He is leading us to. Reaching the home of a friend with whom he was staying, Mr. Gilmore tells us that as he pondered on the blessedness of the divine leadership of God, instinctively there came to him the impulse to write. "I took out my pencil," he says, "and wrote the hymn just as it stands to-day." He afterwards handed it to his wife, and thought no more about it. Praying that God might have a mission for the verses her husband had been inspired to write, Mrs. Gilmore sent the copy, without her husband's knowledge, to a Christian periodical, and there it first appeared in print.

It was thus that the hymn came to the notice of William B. Bradbury, who composed for it the very appropriate tune, with which it has since been associated.

The hymn strikes a bright note of confidence

throughout, and is still a much loved song of praise. In the third verse there is evinced a sustaining power, which, to the weary pilgrim, has proved an unfailing antidote when the road is rough and the sky o'ercast:

> Lord I would clasp Thy hand in mine,
> And never murmur or repine;
> Content, whatever lot I see,
> Since 'tis my God that leadeth me.

ROBERT LOWRY.

ONE evening, about twelve years after Gilmore had written "He leadeth me," another American Baptist minister, whose name to-day takes a high place in the realm of sacred song, was seated at a parlour organ in his home. All that day his thoughts had been dwelling on the glorious triumph of the Resurrection. He was a noted musical composer, and as he sat there, visualizing the wondrous scene, spontaneously there came words and music, giving expression to the thoughts that had been uppermost in his mind:

> Low in the grave He lay,
> Jesus, my Saviour!
> Waiting the coming day,
> Jesus, my Lord.
>
> Up from the grave He arose
> With a mighty triumph o'er His foes;
> He arose a Victor from the dark domain,
> And He lives for ever with His saints to reign!
> He arose! He arose!
> Hallelujah! Christ arose!

HYMNS AND THEIR WRITERS.

The name of the writer of this soul-thrilling Gospel song is Robert Lowry. He was born at Philadelphia, on March 12th, 1826. At the age of seventeen he was brought to the Lord, and after a successful scholastic career at Lewisburg University, he became pastor of the West Chester Baptist Church, Pennsylvania, from which he passed to various important pastorates. Mr. Lowry died at Plainfield, New Jersey, on November 25th, 1899, in his 74th year.

Possibly the best known composition by Dr. Lowry, and one which, it is not improbable, has been sung in most of the Sunday Schools of the world, is the popular children's hymn:

> Shall we gather at the river
> Where bright angel-feet have trod;
> With its crystal tide for ever
> Flowing by the throne of God?

It was written at Brooklyn on a sultry afternoon, in July, 1864, when an epidemic amongst children was raging through the city, bringing death and sorrow into many a home.

Among other popular hymns by the same author, is the pathetic composition, "Where is my wandering boy to-night?" and that old Gospel mission favourite:

> What can wash away my stain?
> Nothing but the blood of Jesus!

A composer of marked ability, Dr. Lowry wrote the music for most of his hymns, besides setting tunes to many others which are widely sung to-day.

E. P. HAMMOND.

ABOUT the time of which we write, a considerable number of Gospel hymns appear to have been written, and not a few came into public favour, due in no small measure to the great Moody and Sankey missions in Great Britain and America, when a notable feature of those stirring times was the prominence given to the ministry of sacred song. The name of E. P. Hammond is better known as a preacher of the Gospel than as a hymn writer, and yet he has left behind a few heavenly lays which may be found in several present-day hymnals. He is the author of the hymn:

> Christians, go and tell of Jesus,
> How He died to save our souls;
> How that He from sin might free us,
> Suffered agonies untold.

This hymn is usually sung to Dr. Lowry's tune which he composed for "Shall we gather at the River?"

Edward Payson Hammond was born at Ellington, Connecticut, September 1st, 1831. He was converted at seventeen, and afterwards devoted himself to the Lord's work, in which he was greatly used on both sides of the Atlantic.

Mr. Hammond compiled and edited several hymnals, which were mostly used in connection with his evangelistic work.

E. P. Hammond's most popular hymn—an especial favourite of C. H. Spurgeon—which has been translated into various languages and sung in many lands, is, "I feel like singing all the time." How this joyous song of praise came into being is an interesting story. Mr. Hammond was conducting a children's service in Utica, New York, and while explaining to the young folks how Jesus loved us and gave Himself for us, he noticed a bright-looking girl burst into tears. When the meeting was over she remained behind, and with others was soon happy in the love of Jesus. The day following, the girl handed Mr. Hammond a letter. "I think I have found the dear Jesus," she wrote, "and I do not see how I could have rejected Him so long. I think I can sing with the rest of those who have found Him, 'Jesus is mine.' The first time I came to the meetings I cried; but now I feel like singing all the time." "This prompted me to write the hymn," says Mr. Hammond when telling the story, "but I had no thought of its ever being sung, although it almost seemed as if I could hear her singing:

> I feel like singing all the time
> My tears are wiped away;
> For Jesus is a Friend of mine,
> I'll serve Him every day.

Mr. George C. Stebbins (whose name is notably associated with so many popular gospel hymns), wrote the bright and appropriate tune to which it has since been sung.

FRANCES RIDLEY HAVERGAL.

> Thou art coming, O my Saviour!
> Coming, God's anointed King!
> Every tongue Thy name confessing,
> Well may we rejoice and sing.

THIS exhilarating Advent hymn was written at the village of Winterdyne in November, 1873, and first appeared in a local newspaper. It was afterwards published in leaflet form with a tune by the authoress—for she was both poet and musician—and very soon came into public favour. The name of Frances Ridley Havergal, its writer, takes a prominent position among the sweet singers of Zion. Her spiritual songs have for more than half-a-century sung themselves into heart and home, till to-day, the echo of their sweet sound may be heard the world over.

Miss Havergal was born on December 14th, 1836, at Astley in Worcestershire, her father, himself the author of several hymns, being at that time vicar of the little parish church there. Very early in life Frances gave evidence of the poetic gift with which she was endowed, and her conversion to God, when yet a girl at school, opened a way to service in this particular sphere, which was willed of God to be a channel of blessing in years to come. Writing to a friend at that time she says: "I committed my soul to the Saviour, and earth and heaven seemed brighter from that moment." This was the young life which many years later was to bequeath to us that sweetest of all consecration hymns, "Take my life, and let it be."

Miss Havergal was a writer who possessed an exceptional faculty for committing to verse words and ideas, almost as quickly as they presented themselves to her cultured mind. A striking example of this is associated with one of her best known hymns, written in 1858, when on a visit to Germany. One day after a long walk, Miss Havergal arrived at the place where she was staying, tired and weary, and seating herself on a sofa, her eyes fell upon a picture on the wall opposite, bearing the words, "I gave my life for thee." Immediately there came to her the overwhelming thought of her Saviour's dying love, and taking up paper and pencil she wrote the whole of the hymn:

> I gave my life for thee;
>   My precious blood I shed,
> That thou might'st ransomed be,
>   And quickened from the dead.
> I gave Myself for thee:
> What hast thou done for Me?

Most of Miss Havergal's hymns were first written on scraps of paper, and afterwards copied into school exercise books, many of which are still preserved. It is interesting to receive her own account of the way in which, in God's hands, she exercised her remarkable gift. "Writing is praying with me; for I never seem to write even a verse by myself, and I feel like a little child writing. You know a child would look up at every sentence and say, 'And what shall I say next?' This is just what I do. I ask that at every line He would give me, not merely thoughts and power, but also every word, even the very rhymes. Very often I have a most distinct and happy consciousness of direct answers." One can readily understand how so many of her messages of song have been so wonderfully used of God, for the writer lived daily in a spiritual atmosphere and in close communion with the Saviour she adored.

Miss Havergal's best loved hymn is of course "Take my life, and let it be." It was written in 1874, and the world-wide favour accorded to this composition is shown by the fact that it has been translated into about a dozen European languages.

> Take my life, and let it be
> Consecrated, Lord, to Thee;
> Take my moments and my days,
> Let them flow in ceaseless praise.
>
> Take my silver and my gold;
> Not a mite would I withhold:
> Take my intellect, and use
> Every power as Thou shalt choose.

Few there are who have sung such words as these, fully realise their deep spiritual meaning more than did the writer herself. But the life of Frances Ridley Havergal was indeed a life of consecration. Thus she wrote to a friend: "The Lord has shown me another little step, and of course I have taken it with extreme delight. 'Take my silver and my gold,' now means shipping off all my ornaments to the Church Missionary House (including a jewel cabinet that is really fit for a countess), where all will be accepted and disposed of for me. I retain a brooch or two for daily wear, which are memorials of my dear parents, also a locket containing a portrait of my dear niece in heaven, my Evelyn, and her two rings; but these I redeem, so that the whole value goes to the Church Missionary Society. Nearly fifty articles are being packed up. I don't think I ever locked a box with such pleasure."

Despite indifferent health, at times aggravated by repeated attacks of illness, Miss Havergal lived a strenuous life, her labours being almost wholly

HYMNS AND THEIR WRITERS.

devoted to the Master's service. "She spoke, she taught, she sang, she prayed, she wrote for Him. She visited the sick and infirm, often undertaking long journeys in order to carry some message of love.

In the autumn of 1878, Miss Havergal made her home at the Mumbles, Swansea Bay. Here, it was hoped would be found a quiet resting-place, that she might recruit some of her lost vitality; but her ever practical compassion toward the poor of the Mumbles overtaxed the invalid's already diminished strength, and on June 3rd of the following year, the sweet singer passed into the presence of the King. She was just forty-two.

Among the many hymns of Frances Ridley Havergal, there is one of especial beauty, "Lord, speak to me, that I may speak," which breathes out the tender longings and aspirations of a sanctified soul, so beautifully exemplified in the life of this saintly writer. Here are the closing verses:

> O give Thine own sweet rest to me,
>   That I may speak with soothing power
> A word in season, as from Thee
>   To weary ones in needful hour.
>
> O fill me with Thy fulness, Lord,
>   Until my very heart o'erflow
> In kindling thought, and glowing word,
>   Thy love to tell, Thy praise to show.
>
> O use me, Lord, use even me,
>   Just as Thou wilt, and when, and where;
> Until Thy blessed face I see,
>   Thy rest, Thy joy, Thy glory share.

FANNY CROSBY.

> I am Thine, O Lord! I have heard Thy voice,
> And it told Thy love to me;
> But I long to rise in the arms of faith,
> And be closer drawn to Thee.

NO other lady writer in the whole realm of hymnody has given to the world so many gems of sacred song, which have attained such a high degree of usefulness and popularity, as Frances Jane Crosby.

Fanny was born in the town of Southeast, Putnam County, New York, on March 24th, 1820. When six weeks old she suffered the loss of her sight through what appeared to be an unfortunate mistake perpetrated by their family physician, in his treatment of a slight cold which had caused inflammation of the eyes. "But," says the blind hymn writer when speaking of the calamity in later years, "I have not for a moment, in more than eighty-five years, felt a spark of resentment against him; for I have always believed that the good Lord, in His infinite mercy, by this means consecrated me to the work which I am still permitted to do. When I remember how I have been blessed, how can I repine? Darkness may throw a shadow over my outer vision, but there is no cloud that can keep the sunlight of hope from a trustful soul." What a beautiful testimony! Can we wonder why God has so signally used the hymns of this saintly woman?

When Fanny was fifteen she made the long journey of over a thousand miles to New York Institution for the Blind, where she remained for twenty-three years, first as a pupil and later as a teacher. It was here that she met Alexander

HYMNS AND THEIR WRITERS.

Van Alstyne, whom she married in 1858. After her marriage it was her husband's wish that her literary name, Fanny J. Crosby, should still be used, as it had already become known to the public, through her poems.

At an early age the faculty of verse-making manifested itself in the life of the little blind girl who, being endowed with a keen poetic mind, soon began to write in earnest, and her first volume of poems was published when she was quite a young woman, receiving the high approbation of no less a literary critic than William Cullen Bryant, the celebrated American poet.

It was not, however, till she had reached the age of forty-three that Fanny Crosby commenced writing hymns. This came about by her introduction to William B. Bradbury (known as the Father of Sacred Song), who invited her to write words to some melodies he had composed. The first she wrote for him was the missionary hymn, "There's a cry from Macedonia." Thus began Fanny Crosby's work as a writer of Gospel hymns.

The words of many of her hymns were composed to suit the tunes supplied to her, as in the well-known instance of "Safe in the arms of Jesus," which was written in less than half-an-hour, after hearing the melody played on a small organ by her friend Dr. W. H. Doane the composer. On another occasion Dr. Doane came to the blind hymn writer with a tune, requesting her to write a hymn about "Every day and hour." She responded with the words of that beautiful hymn:

> Saviour, more than life to me,
> I am clinging, clinging close to Thee;
> Let Thy precious blood applied,
> Keep me ever, ever near Thy side.

> Every day, every hour,
> Let me know Thy cleansing power;
> May Thy tender love to me
> Bind me closer, closer, Lord, to Thee.

The hymn "I shall know Him," had its origin under similar circumstances. Mr. John R. Sweney, the composer of many of Sankey's favourite hymns, sent a melody to Fanny with the request that she might write something "tender and sympathetic." "I prayed that appropriate words might be given me for the music," she wrote when recalling the story; "and the train of thought led me to the sweet consciousness that I shall know my Saviour 'by the print of the nails in His hand.'" Thus came the words:

> When my life work is ended and I cross the swelling tide,
> When the bright and glorious morning I shall see;
> I shall know my Redeemer when I reach the other side,
> And His smile will be the first to welcome me.
>
> I shall know Him, I shall know Him,
> When redeemed by His side I shall stand;
> I shall know Him, I shall know Him,
> By the print of the nails in His hand.

Among Fanny Crosby's hymns, "Saved by Grace," which was written when she was in her seventy-second year, takes a high place in the affections of Christians the world over. It had its origin in a little prayer meeting, at the close of which she was asked to write a hymn on "Grace," this having been the theme of the meeting. The same night, before retiring to rest, she found expression in the words of the hymn so much beloved:

> Some day the silver cord will break,
> And I no more, as now shall sing!
> But oh, the joy when I shall wake
> Within the palace of the King!
> And I shall see Him face to face
> And tell the story saved by grace.

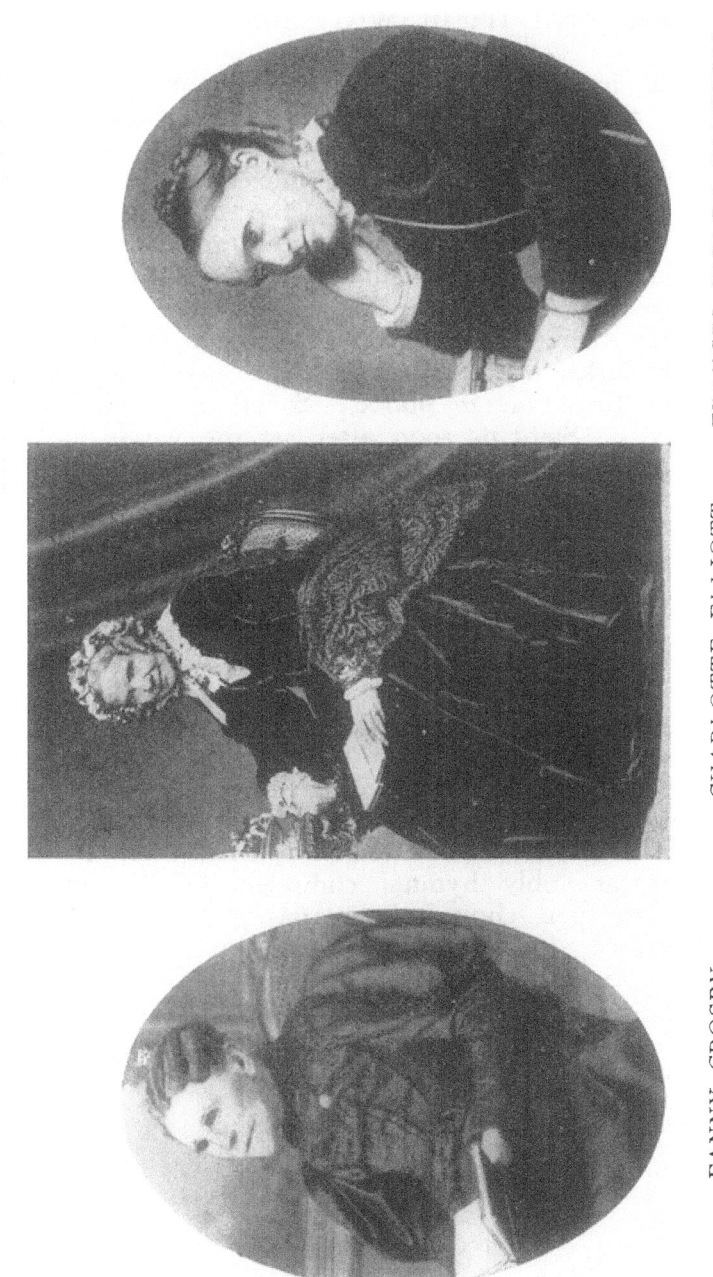

FANNY CROSBY.   CHARLOTTE ELLIOTT.   FRANCES RIDLEY HAVERGAL

HYMNS AND THEIR WRITERS. 179

The circumstances of its introduction to the public are interesting. A year or two after the hymn was written Fanny happened to attend a conference at Northfield, at which Mr. Ira D. Sankey was present. Seeing the blind hymn writer in the audience, a request was sent in by some of those present that they wished to hear her speak. At first she begged to be excused, but Mr. Sankey prevailed upon her to make a few remarks, at the close of which she recited, for the first time in public, "Saved by Grace. George C. Stebbins soon after set the words to the beautiful tune to which it has since been sung.

Fanny Crosby was both a prolific and rapid writer, many of her hymns being composed in a few minutes, with very little effort. Endowed with a singularly retentive memory, the blind poetess rarely repeated herself in the wide range of her 8,000 hymns.

Frances Jane Crosby laid down her pen on February 12th, 1915, and entered into the presence of the King, at the advanced age of ninety-five.

Besides the hymns "I am Thine, O Lord, and "Saviour more than life to me," already quoted, assembly hymnal compilers have been happy in their choice of several others equally well-known including: "Praise Him! Praise Him!" "Safe in the arms of Jesus," "Thou my everlasting portion," "Take the world but give me Jesus," and that sweetest of all prayer-meeting hymns:

'Tis the blessed hour of prayer, when our hearts lowly bend,
And we gather to Jesus, our Saviour and Friend;
If we come to Him in faith, His protection to share,
What a balm for the weary! O how sweet to be there!

MARY J. WALKER.

> O spotless Lamb of God, in Thee
> Thy Father's holiness we see;
> And with delight Thy children trace,
> In Thee, His wondrous love and grace.
>
> When we behold Thee, Lamb of God,
> Beneath our sin's tremendous load,
> Expiring on the accursèd tree,
> How great our guilt with grief we see.

THIS beautiful hymn is from the pen of Mrs. M. J. Walker, a younger sister of James G. Deck, whose name is so notably associated with Brethren hymnology. Mary Jane Deck was born on April 27th, 1816, and at the age of thirty-two was married to Dr. Edward Walker of Cheltenham, a godly and consistent Christian with pronounced evangelical convictions, who was at that time incumbent of St. Mary's Parish Church. Many of Mrs. Walker's hymns made their first appearance as leaflets, but were later included in a collection known as "Psalms and Hymns for Public and Social Worship," published by Dr. Walker in 1855. From this source the hymns of this gifted writer first received prominence, and have since been freely copied into various hymnals. At the age of twenty-nine Miss Deck (as she then was) wrote the hymn commencing:

> The wanderer no more will roam,
> The lost one to the fold hath come,
> The prodigal is welcomed home
>   O Lamb of God, in Thee!

It was written at the suggestion of her brother, J. G. Deck, who happened to remark that the manner of God's love in receiving us needed to be known, as well as our way of coming to Him. This composition was really meant to be complimentary to Charlotte Elliott's hymn "Just as I am," which was written nine years previous to this time, and had already come into public favour. The second verse gives full expression to the thought which prompted the hymn, and conveys a fitting picture of the Father's love at the return of His wayward child:

> Though clad in rags, by sin defiled,
> The Father hath embraced His child;
> And I am pardoned, reconciled,
> O Lamb of God, in Thee!

After the death of her husband in 1872, Mrs. Walker spent the remaining years of her life in fellowship with those believers with whom she had previously been in sympathy. She died at Cheltenham on July 2nd, 1878.

Mrs. Walker is the author of the poem "I have Christ—What want I more?" which has been set to music and used as a hymn. She also gave to us the hymn commencing:

> I journey through a desert drear and wild,
> Yet in my heart by such sweet thoughts beguiled
> Of Him on Whom I lean, my Strength, my Stay,
> I can forget the sorrows of the way.

Mrs. Walker wrote many beautiful hymns and poems, but the one composition from her pen which has gained unbounded favour almost since the day it was written, and has been used in bringing many souls into the Kingdom of God, is the hymn "Jesus I will trust Thee."

In his delightfully written Life Story, Mr. Sankey narrates an interesting story regarding this hymn. Major D. W. Whittle, himself the author of many well-known hymns and a colleague of Sankey, was conducting Gospel meetings in Belfast. One night, at the close of a searching address, Major Whittle observed a man lingering behind. On approaching him the evangelist found that he was a merchant in the city. The man appeared to be in deep distress of soul because of his sins, and the preacher sought to point him to "the Lamb of God which taketh away the sin of the world." It was very evident that a struggle was going on in his soul, the powers for good and evil striving for the mastery. "We went down on our knees and prayed," said Major Whittle when relating the incident, "Then after a while the anxious one straightened himself up, and gave vent to his feelings in this hymn, for he was a capital singer:

> Jesus I will trust Thee,
> Trust Thee with my soul!
> Guilty, lost, and helpless,
> Thou canst make me whole.

It was indeed a song of victory over Satan, and a song of praise to Christ his Saviour.

This hymn was a favourite of Frances Ridley Havergal, and it is said that the words of the first verse were among the last that came from the lips of the sweet singer, a few minutes before she passed away.

Among the numerous hymns which have engaged one's attention for many years, "Jesus I will trust Thee" occupies a treasured place in the heart, and the mention of it here, recalls an event which shall ever remain fresh while memory shall last. Even now, after the passing of more than thirty years, there is clearly depicted in the mind, an old-fashioned Gospel meeting in a dimly lighted room at the head of a wooden stair, on a cold October night. At this present moment, now far removed from the memorable event, nothing that the preacher said during the service can be recalled; but the singing of that hymn at the close of the meeting was the means of bringing about a decision, which, ere the clock struck the midnight hour, culminated in the conversion to God of a young life. That night, with joy unspeakable, and resting my all on the blessed assurance of eternal salvation revealed in the words of Romans ten and nine, I was able to sing from the heart:

> Jesus, I do trust Thee,
>   Trust Thee without doubt;
> "Whosoever cometh"
>   Thou "wilt not cast out";
> Faithful is Thy promise,
>   Precious is Thy blood—
> These my soul's salvation,
>   Thou my Saviour God.

ANNE STEELE.

> Father of mercies! in Thy Word,
>   What endless glory shines!
> For ever be Thy Name adored
>   For these celestial lines.

SOME of the choicest gems of heavenly song have had their birth in the sick chamber. Miss Anne Steele, the writer of this hymn—the original of which contains twelve verses—was an invalid, and the greater part of her life was spent in enforced confinement to her room. She was born in 1716, at the village of Broughton, in Hampshire, where her father, a timber merchant, regularly officiated as pastor of a Baptist church.

Reared in a spiritual atmosphere, Anne Steele very soon opened her heart to receive the Saviour, and at the age of fourteen she confessed her faith in Christ by being publicly baptised. Endowed with a taste for literature she commenced writing at an early age, but it was not until later in life that she could be prevailed upon to publish her various compositions.

The shadow of a tragic event, which occurred when Anne Steele was quite a young woman, rarely left her, and at times revealed itself in the plaintive tone of many of her sacred poems. Her betrothed, a young man of promise and ability, was accidentally drowned while bathing, not long before the day arranged for the wedding; and at the very time when the two should have been joined together as husband and wife, his lifeless body, which had been recovered from the river, was carried home. It was following this sad event that Anne Steele penned one of our sweetest resignation hymns:

> When I survey life's varied scene,
>   Amid the darkest hours,
> Sweet rays of comfort shine between,
>   And thorns are mixed with flowers.
>
> Thy powerful Word supports my hope,
>   Sweet cordial to the mind,
> And bears my fainting spirit up,
>   And bids me wait resigned.

She never fully recovered from the shock sustained by her great loss, which accentuated an already enfeebled health, brought about by a slight accident in girlhood, and the remainder of her life was spent in retirement.

Miss Steele is claimed to be the first Englishwoman who takes a permanent place amongst hymn writers, and has been referred to as the Frances Ridley Havergal of the eighteenth century.

For more than a hundred years, her hymns—which were usually written over the nom-de-plume of "Theodosia"—have been in extensive use, and a goodly number are still in general favour to-day. Anne Steele passed away in 1778, at the age of sixty-one.

Besides "Father of Mercies," which is perhaps her best known hymn, other compositions by Miss Steele with which we are familiar are, "Thy gracious presence, O our God," "Father, whate'er of earthly bliss," and the one commencing:

> He lives—the great Redeemer lives;
> What joy the blest assurance gives!
> And now before His Father, God,
> Pleads the full merit of His blood.

CHARLOTTE ELLIOTT.

ANOTHER "shut-in" writer whose name in the realm of hymnody takes a high place, is Charlotte Elliott. She was born at Clapham, in 1789. From her earliest years, through weakness and ill-health she was precluded from sharing in the many activities of life; and yet, although rarely free from pain, she was ever bright and cheerful, for Charlotte Elliott had come to realise that the quiet of her sick chamber was to be her own special sphere of labour. And from this obscure place, away from the glare of publicity, there went forth songful messages, which found lodgment in the hearts of multitudes the world over.

Best known of all the compositions of this gifted authoress, is the tender and appealing hymn:

> Just as I am, without one plea,
> But that Thy blood was shed for me,
> And that Thou bidst me come to Thee—
> O Lamb of God, I come!

Written when Miss Elliott was forty-five years old, this hymn has been translated into almost every European language, and is to be found in practically every collection of Christian hymns. So many fanciful stories have been woven around the birth of this famous hymn, that it is refreshing to learn the true history of how "Just as I am" came into being. The story has been told by the late Dr. Moule, Bishop of Durham, whose wife was a close relative of the hymn writer.

"Charlotte Elliott was living at Brighton with a married brother, a clergyman, the Rev. Henry Venn Elliott. The whole family had gone off to a bazaar in which they were greatly interested; and the frail invalid had been left at home alone, lying on a sofa, with her heart a little sad at being, as usual, shut out from all good works. For her own comfort she began to ponder on the grand certainties of salvation—her Lord, His power and His promises. Then came a sudden feeling of peace and contentment, and taking her pen, she wrote the beautiful verses of 'Just as I am.' Surely they were God-given—a precious and priceless gift indeed—from her Heavenly Father to His chastened and much-loved child. As the day wore on, her sister-in-law, Mrs. H. V. Elliott, came in to see her and bring news of the bazaar. She read the hymn and asked for a copy. So the hymn first stole out from that quiet room into the world, where since that day it has

HYMNS AND THEIR WRITERS.

been sowing and reaping till a multitude which only God can number have been blessed through its message."

It is said that after Miss Elliott's death, a locked box, discovered among her belongings, when opened, was found to contain over 1,000 letters which the authoress had received from grateful writers to whom her hymn, "Just as I am," had been a blessing. Charlotte Elliott lived to the advanced age of eighty-two, and died at Brighton on the evening of September 22nd, 1871.

We cannot leave this hymn without quoting the last verse: words which are still fragrant with memories of wonderful times of revival.

> Just as I am, Thy love unknown
> Has broken every barrier down;
> Now to be Thine, yea, Thine alone—
> O Lamb of God, I come!

Possibly the next best known hymn by Charlotte Elliott is, "My God, my Father, while I stray," which had its origin following the death of her younger brother, with whom, for a time, she made her home. They were greatly attached to each other, and though his death cast a shadow over the closing years of her life, the bereaved authoress breathes the true spirit of resignation in the lines:

> My God, my Father, while I stray
> Far from my home, in life's rough way,
> O teach me from my heart to say,
>   "Thy will be done."
>
> If dark my path and hard my lot,
> May I be still and murmur not;
> But breathe the prayer divinely taught,
>   "Thy will be done."

MARGARET L. CARSON.

> My chains are snapt, the bonds of sin are broken,
>   And I am free;
> O let the triumphs of His grace be spoken,
>   Who died for me.

MARGARET LEDLEY CARSON, the writer of this hymn, was the daughter of Dr. G. L. Carson, a medical practitioner of Coleraine, Ireland, where she was born in 1833. The early days of her Christian life were marked by a deep spirituality, influenced no doubt, by her intimate association at that time with such stalwarts of the truth as J. N. Darby and C. H. Mackintosh; the latter for many years being her close friend and helper.

During the great revival of 1859 Miss Carson became an active worker, and being a woman of remarkable personality and keen spiritual perception, she was used in winning many trophies of grace for the Master.

The date of "My chains are snapt," reveals the fact that it was written when the authoress was quite a young woman, and was thus among her first compositions. Soon after committing the verses to her notebook, Miss Carson showed the hymn to her friend C. H. Mackintosh, soliciting his criticism. After reading the verses through, Mr. Mackintosh suggested that the hymn only lacked one thing, and that was the theme of the Lord's second coming; and taking his pencil he added the last verse:

> We wait to see the Morning Star appearing
>   In Glory bright;
> This blessed hope illumes, with beams most cheering
>   The hours of night.

EMMA FRANCES BEVAN.

MARGARET LEDLEY CARSON.

Miss Carson was of an amiable and cheerful disposition, and being possessed of some means, she was able to devote the greater part of a long and useful life to aggressive work for God. "In schoolhouse, or mission hall, or soldiers' home," writes one who knew Miss Carson well, "She was ever diligent in the Lord's work. She was also a tactful and able worker in dealing with individuals, and there are many living to-day, known to the writer, who passed from death to life in her drawing-room."

Ever a generous giver, Miss Carson built a Gospel hall at Portrush, so that believers might meet for the breaking of bread; and many happy times were spent around the Lord's table with Christians from many parts of the kingdom. It was here she spent the closing years of her life.

Miss Carson passed away on February 24th, 1920, at the age of 87 years.

ELIZABETH CODNER.

THERE are many instances on record where the singing of a hymn has arrested a wayward soul, and been the means of turning the feet of the wanderer from the paths of sin. A striking illustration of this occurred during a mission in the West End of London. The hymn which was used of God is one of tender appeal:

> Lord! to Thee my heart, ascending,
> For Thy mercy full and free,
> Thankful sings for grace transcending,
> Grace vouchsafed to sinful me—
> Even me!

A young lady who was a familiar figure in fashionable circles, and had led a very worldly life, was prevailed upon to attend one of the meetings. Apparently untouched by the faithful message of the preacher, she rose to go at the close of the service. As she moved slowly down the crowded aisle, her attention was arrested by the words of the hymn sung by those who remained behind for the after-meeting. Just as the young lady approached the door they were singing the last verse:

> Pass me not! Thy lost one bringing,
> Bind my heart, O Lord to Thee!
> While the streams of life are springing,
> Blessing others, oh, bless me!
> Even me!

The words went straight to her heart, and all the way home there kept ringing in her ears the conviction "You are the lost one." Reaching home, she sought the quietude of her bedroom, where, in agony of soul, she sobbed out the prayer from the depths of her heart.

> "Pass me not! Thy lost one bringing!"

Then she remembered how she had read somewhere that the Son of Man had come to seek and save that which was lost. The cry of the lost one was heard, that night the burden rolled away, and the penitent one found peace for her troubled soul, by trusting in the atoning work of Calvary.

This hymn, which had its birth about the year following the '59 revival in Ireland, was written by Mrs. Elizabeth Codner, and it first appeared in print in 1861. The circumstances of its origin are worthy of relating. Several members of her Bible Class for whom

HYMNS AND THEIR WRITERS. 191

she had prayed, and over whom she was watching with anxious hope, attended a meeting at which details were given of the wonderful spiritual blessing which had swept over the country. They were greatly impressed with what they heard, and Mrs. Codner pressed upon them the privilege of sharing in the blessing. On the Sunday following, not being well enough to attend the class, she had a time of quiet communion with the Lord. "Those young people were still on my heart," says Mrs. Codner, "and I longed to press upon them an individual appeal. Without effort, words seemed to be given to me, and they took the form of a hymn. I had no thought of sending it beyond the limits of my own circle, but, passing it on to one and another, it became a word of power, and I then published it as a leaflet."

Since then Mrs. Codner's hymn has had a wonderful history, and is to be found in most of the present-day hymnals.

The verses of this hymn which are given in the "Believers Hymn Book"—obviously because of the particular object of this collection—are different to those in general use, the last verse, already quoted, not being given.

The tune, which is by Mr. W. B. Bradbury, is arranged so that the burden of the song, "Even me," is repeated as a refrain, giving just the desired effect to a pleasing and appropriate melody.

MARY PETERS.

> Around Thy table, holy Lord,
> In fellowship we meet,
> Obedient to Thy gracious Word,
> This feast of love to eat.

THIS beautiful communion hymn, which has long claimed a treasured place in our affections because of its many hallowed associations with the "sweet feast of love divine," was written by the wife of a country parson, and first appeared in a collection of hymns used by Brethren, which was published in London in 1842.

Mary Peters, the writer, was the daughter of Richard Bowly, and was born at Cirencester in 1813. She subsequently married John Peters, some time rector of Quennington, Gloucestershire; and in the quietude of the old Rectory many of the hymns of Mary Peters were written.

Of the many compositions by this gifted writer, "Around Thy table, holy Lord" is the shortest, and certainly one of the sweetest.

It is hardly necessary to state that not the least important feature of a hymn for congregational use is its tune. To enjoy to the full this song of supplication is to join in the singing of it to the fine old tune "Wiltshire," a melody so closely associated with the Twenty-Third Psalm, and yet eminently suited to give expression to the theme conveyed in the words of this choice composition.

Another hymn of singular beauty by the same author, begins:

> O Lord, how much Thy Name unfolds
> To every opened ear;
> The pardoned sinner's memory holds
> None other half so dear.

> Jesus! it speaks a life of love,
> Of sorrows meekly borne;
> It tells of sympathy above,
> Whatever griefs we mourn.

Other hymns by this writer, familiar to most of us, are "The holiest now we enter," "Praise ye the Lord, again, again," "Through the love of God our Saviour," and "O blessed Lord, what hast Thou done!"

Mary Peters died at Clifton, Bristol, on July 29th, 1856.

The most ambitious literary work of Mrs. Peters was a history of the world from the Creation to the accession of Queen Victoria, published in seven volumes, which must have engaged the close attention of the author for a considerable period. And yet, with the march of time, while this notable addition to historic literature has now become a back number, the hymns of Mary Peters have lost none of their old-time sweetness, and are to be found in the hymnals of almost every Christian denomination.

JANE CREWDSON.

THE seclusion of the sick room has been the birthplace of many of our choicest hymns. There the secret of God's power and the influence of the Holy Spirit have been felt and realised by the writer, to the exclusion of everything else, producing upon the poetic vision thought and word in happy sequence. Thus in the exercise of such God-given songs the singer experiences in a peculiar way the tender touch of the Spirit-filled writer, or is thrilled to ecstasy by the song's joyous note of praise.

It was from the sick chamber of an invalid lady that we received such tender and enduring lines as these:

> O for the peace that floweth as a river!
> Making life's desert places bloom and smile;
> O for the faith to grasp heaven's bright "for ever!"
> Amid the shadows of earth's "little while."

This hymn was written by Mrs. Jane Crewdson. It first appeared in a small volume under the title of "A Little While, and other poems," published the year after the death of the author, which took place at Summerlands, near Manchester, in 1863, she being in her fifty-fourth year. From this collection, which passed through several editions, many of the gifted writer's hymns came into general use. The preface to the little book of poems, written by an intimate friend, says: "The author's mind was singularly varied; she was thus qualified to meet the need of others, and to lead them to the Source and Centre whence she derived her brightness in shadowy places, her cheerfulness in pain, and her unfailing joy and peace in believing. It was her delight to minister to their spirit wants out of her rich sympathies. Perhaps she may still be admitted through the medium of these pages, into fellowship with many a troubled heart; and may such, like her, find 'rest in Jesus.'"

Other hymns by Jane Crewdson, with which the reader is familiar, are: "O Saviour, I have nought to plead," written a short time before the writer's home-call; "I've found a joy in sorrow," and that hymn of thanksgiving and resignation which gives to us a glimpse of her devout and prayerful spirit, "O Thou, whose bounty fills our cup." The date of this hymn is given as 1860, a time when Mrs. Crewdson was passing through much sickness and trial. And yet she was able to write:

> O Thou, whose bounty fills our cup
>   With every blessing meet!
> We give Thee thanks for every drop,
>   The bitter and the sweet.
>
> We thank Thee for the desert road
>   And for the river side;
> For all Thy goodness has bestowed,
>   And all Thy grace denied.

MARY SHEKLETON.

ANOTHER writer confined to her couch gave to us that devotional hymn, "It passeth knowledge, that dear love of Thine." Though a confirmed invalid, Mary Shekleton was ever busy with her pen, and from her home in Dublin she sent forth her messages, influencing many a heart by her poems and other quiet ministries of love. Of this writer, Frances Ridley Havergal once wrote: "She was one of the many faithful sofa workers who do what they can, and beyond that are content to wait."

Miss Shekleton formed what became known as "The Invalids' Prayer Union," which made a bond of union with Christians not only in her native land but in many parts of the world. She died in Dublin, on September 28th, 1883.

The hymns of Mary Shekleton are few in number, but they breathe out that compassion and love for the Saviour so fragrantly expressed in the words of her best known hymn:

> It passeth knowledge, that dear love of Thine,
> Lord Jesus, Saviour; yet this soul of mine
> Would of Thy love, in all its breadth and length,
> Its height and depth, its everlasting strength,
>   Know more and more.

ANNE R. COUSIN.

> Oh! Christ, He is the fountain,
> The deep sweet well of love;
> The streams on earth I've tasted,
> More deep I'll drink above.
> There, to an ocean fulness
> His mercy doth expand,
> And glory, glory dwelleth,
> In Immanuel's land.

BETWEEN fifty and sixty years ago a modest-looking volume of devotional verse was published bearing the title "Immanuel's Land and Other Pieces," by A. R. C. The authoress who thus announced herself was Anne R. Cousin. She lived to the ripe age of four-score years and two, but long before her home-call she had the satisfaction of knowing that two of the pieces in her little book had found a place in a large number of hymn books, and that at least one of them was a popular favourite.

The piece which gives title to the volume is now better known as the hymn beginning "The Sands of Time are Sinking"; while another which she entitled "The Substitute," appears in most hymn books as "O, Christ what burdens bowed Thy head!"

Mrs. Cousin was a daughter of Dr. David Ross Cundell of Leith, and was born in 1824. Her father served in the British army for several years, as a surgeon, and was present at the Battle of Waterloo with the 33rd Regiment. After the peace of 1816, Dr. Cundell settled in his native town, Leith, where he died when his only child was just three years old. Mrs. Cundell, after her husband's death, removed to Edinburgh, where she resided until her daughter's marriage, in 1847, to the Rev. William Cousin, then minister of Chelsea Presbyterian Church, London, but who had previously been minister at Duns, Berwickshire. Shortly after her marriage, Mrs. Cousin removed with her husband to the Free Church of Irvine, and it was there, about the year 1856, that she composed her best known hymn, "The Sands of Time are Sinking," a hymn which is now known and used throughout the English-speaking world.

The hymn is a selection from a poem of nineteen verses, inspired by a long and loving study of the "Life and Letters of Samuel Rutherford," and founded on the Scottish martyr's dying words, "Glory dwelleth in Immanuel's land." A song of heaven, it deservedly takes high rank, for no other hymn on this theme—so dear to the Christian heart—expresses with such emphasis, the secret joy of heaven's attraction: the glory of the Lamb that was slain.

The pathetic interest of this hymn arises from the story which it tells, and which is one of the memorable events in Scottish history. The cruel persecution meted out to the saintly Rutherford has been ineffacably recorded in the annals of the Scottish Covenanters. Though condemned to die, his threatened fate was averted by his death in prison. He was born about 1600, at the village of Nisbet, in Roxburghshire. The name of Samuel Rutherford will always be associated with "fair Anwoth on the Solway," where for many years he faithfully and fearlessly ministered the Word of God. "On the 27th July, 1636, he was cited before the High Commission Court to answer for his nonconformity to the acts of Episcopsy and his work against the Arminians." This cost him his Kirk and Manse at Anwoth, and he was banished to Aberdeen. Two years later, the Covenanters being successful, he returned to Anwoth, and the following year was made professor at St. Andrews. The Restoration brought Rutherford further persecution. He was again deprived of his offices and a charge of high treason was brought against him. But while the citation was pending there was a more imperative citation served, and in his answer to the demand for his presence, he sent the message: "I am summoned before a higher Judge and judicatory; that first summons I behove to answer; and, ere a few days arrive, I shall be where few kings and great folks come." And from the dark and cheerless dungeon of the St Andrews prison, Samuel Rutherford passed to the glory of Immanuel's Land, on March 20th, 1661. His anticipations were realised; the "summer morn" he longed for had come at last. For, long ere the shadows began to gather, his heart told forth in a joyous and expectant note, the thought which clothes the celestial words—

> The bride eyes not her garment,
> But her dear bridegroom's face;
> I will not gaze at glory,
> But on the King of grace.
> Not at the crown he giveth,
> But on his piercèd hand;
> The Lamb is all the glory
> Of Immanuel's land.

In "The Believers Hymn Book," possibly for the sake of brevity, the first verse, by which the hymn is best known, has been omitted. The lines have a sweet familiarity:

> The sands of time are sinking,
> The dawn of heaven breaks,
> The summer morn I've sighed for,
> The fair, sweet morn awakes.

HYMNS AND THEIR WRITERS.

> Dark, dark has been the midnight,
> But dayspring is at hand,
> And glory, glory dwelleth
> In Immanuel's land.

So varied are the subjects of the different hymns, and so many hallowed associations cling to a hymn here and there, which gives this and that one a pre-eminent place in our thoughts, that it is never an easy matter to express an opinion as to the best hymn in any particular hymnal. It is safe to state, however, that among the ten best hymns in use among the various assemblies, this hymn takes a very high place.

Dr. John G. Paton, of the New Hebrides, in a letter to the authoress, tells of the profound impression it made upon his mind when sung by a large congregation in St. Kilda, Australia, as the old year was passing away and the new year coming in.

Mrs. Cousin is the author of that tender hymn:

> When we reach our peaceful dwelling
> On the strong eternal hills.

The other hymn already referred to has been much used, particularly in home mission work, and was greatly loved by Mr. Sankey, who spoke of it as a hymn "very much blessed." Here is the first verse:—

> O Christ, what burdens bowed Thy head!
> Our load was laid on Thee;
> Thou stoodest in the sinner's stead—
> Bear'st all my ill for me:
> A victim led, Thy blood was shed;
> Now there's no load for me.

In 1860, Mrs. Cousin and her husband removed to the Free Church, Melrose, in which town they resided for eighteen years, living afterwards in Edinburgh, where the gifted authoress died on December 6th, 1906.

MARIANNE NUNN.

> One there is above all others;
> O how He loves!
> His is love beyond a brother's;
> O how He loves!
> Earthly friends may fail or leave us,
> One day soothe, the next day grieve us,
> But this Friend will ne'er deceive us—
> O how He loves!

THE name of the writer of this hymn is Miss Marianne Nunn. She was born at Colchester in 1779, and during the greater part of her life lived in retirement. Thus in the quietude of her home, the facile pen of the writer gave eloquent expression of her inmost feelings as she meditated upon the constant and unfailing love of the "Friend that sticketh closer than a brother." And so the hymn by which her name is remembered was sent forth.

"O how He loves!" was originally set to an old Welsh tune "Ar hy-d y nos," and first appeared in a collection of hymns published by the author's brother in 1817. Since then the hymn has undergone several changes at the hands of compilers, but its popularity has not in any measure diminished, and is still widely used, especially amongst the young.

The author was sister to John and William Nunn, both of whom left a few hymns which are still in use.

Marianne Nunn died in 1847.

JANE E. LEESON.

THE writer of the following hymn was Jane E. Leeson:

> Have ye counted the cost,
> Have ye counted the cost,
>   Ye warriors of the Cross?
> Are ye fixed in heart for your Master's sake,
>   To suffer all earthly loss?

SHE was born in 1807, and died in 1882. Very little is known of Miss Leeson's personal history, but she has contributed to the ever increasing Songs of Zion many beautiful hymns, besides having produced other literary works. A notable example is her "Paraphrases and Hymns for Congregational Singing"—published in 1853 —a considerable number of which have been arranged from the Scottish Paraphrases. This collection included many of her own original compositions.

Miss Leeson's best known hymn was written for children, and is still a favourite—

> Loving Shepherd of Thy sheep,
> Keep me, Lord, in safety keep;
> Nothing can Thy power withstand,
> None can pluck me from Thy hand.

JANE E. HALL.

Among the many favourite pieces contributed to Sankey's "Sacred Songs and Solos," which find a place in our hymn books is the one beginning:

> The love that Jesus had for me,
> To suffer on the cruel tree,
> That I a ransomed soul might be,
>   Is more than tongue can tell!

It was written by an American lady, Jane E. Hall, of Battleborough, Vermont, about fifty years ago. The hymn is wedded to a pleasing and appropriate tune composed by the author herself, which has contributed in no small measure to the hymn's popularity and usefulness.

AMELIA M. HULL.

AMELIA MATILDA HULL, the author of "I have been at the Altar," was not a prolific writer, but she wrote at least one hymn, which, almost since its birth, has taken a prominent place amongst the Gospel songs of the last half century. And it is doubtful whether the name of the author would have been remembered as a hymn writer but for this one composition:

> There is life for a look at the Crucified One,
>   There is life at this moment for thee;
> Then look, sinner, look unto Him and be saved,
>   Unto Him who was nailed to the tree.

Miss Hull was born at Marpool Hall, Exmouth, in 1825, and was sister to Captain Hull, a notable figure in the early days of Brethren. She lived a life of devotion, self-sacrifice and whole-heartedness in the cause of Christ, and passed into the presence of her Lord in 1882.

LADY CAMPBELL.

MANY beautiful hymns penned in a moment of inspiration, which were never intended to pass beyond the stage of manuscript, have, when taken up and placed in a permanent collection, found a channel of blessing in the Church.

The hymns of Lady Campbell, though not very numerous, were first printed in lithograph from the author's manuscript, for private circulation. In this form her best known hymn, of which the opening verse is here given, received introduction:

> Praise ye Jehovah! Praise the Lord most holy,
>   Who cheers the contrite, girds with strength the weak;
> Praise Him who will with glory crown the lowly,
>   And with salvation beautify the meek.

It was written during the Christmas week of 1838. Four years later the hymn appeared in J. G. Deck's "Psalms, Hymns and Spiritual Songs," and from this source it has passed into a large number of hymn books.

Lady Campbell was the eldest daughter of General Sir John Malcolm, G.C.B., a distinguished soldier and diplomat. In 1827 she was married to Sir Alexander Thomas Cockburn-Campbell, Bart., one of the early Brethren, a man of sterling character who ever sought to manifest a life of humility and unselfishness. It is said that in his zeal for a return to primitive Christian simplicity, he insisted that the household servants should daily dine with his wife and himself. On one occasion Sir Alexander arrived late for dinner and was rather surprised to find the meal already far advanced. The servants did not appear to be much abashed, and explained that as he was late they could not wait, and so had begun without him!

Most of Lady Campbell's hymns are to be found in Brethren hymnals, while a few have come into general use.

CHARITIE L. BANCROFT.

A HYMN which bears the title of "Heavenly Anticipation" in the author's original copy has attained much favour, not only in this country but also in America. It begins:

> O for the robes of whiteness,
> O for the tearless eyes;
> O for the glorious brightness
> Of the unclouded skies!
> O for the no more weeping
> Within the land of love;
> The endless joy of keeping
> The bridal feast above!

Written during the wonderful spiritual revival of 1859-60 in the north of Ireland, by a girl not yet out of her teens, it was indeed the soul's expression of a "first love"; for the girl had but recently found the Saviour.

"O for the robes of whiteness" was first published in leaflet form, but soon afterwards found its way into several collections. Charitie Lee Bancroft, nee Smith, the author, was the daughter of Dr. Sidney Smith, Rector of Drumragh, County Tyrone, Ireland, and was born at Bloomfield, Merrion, near Dublin, in 1841. She was married in 1869 to Arthur E. Bancroft. Many of Mrs. Bancroft's compositions made their first appearance in periodicals. In 1867, her poems and hymns were collected and sent forth in a little volume entitled "Within the Veil." From this collection many of Mrs. Bancroft's best known hymns have been selected, including:

> Before the throne of God above,
> I have a strong, a perfect plea—
> A great High Priest, whose name is Love,
> Who ever lives and pleads for me.

ELIZABETH C. D. CLEPHANE.

WHEN Miss Clephane, at the request of a friend, wrote a few verses for a children's magazine, she little thought that, years after she had passed away, the poem would be taken up, set to music, and sung in almost every English-speaking country of the world. But such was the case.

It was during the Moody and Sankey mission to this country in 1873-74, that the two American evangelists, while travelling from Glasgow to Edinburgh, happened to observe the little poem, which had been reprinted in a newspaper. Greatly struck by the verses, Sankey read them over to his colleague, afterwards cutting out the poem and puting it away in his pocket.

Soon afterwards, at the close of an impressive address on "The Good Shepherd," given in the Free Church Assembly Hall, Edinburgh, Moody turned to Sankey and asked him to sing something in keeping with his subject. For a moment Sankey was unable to think of a suitable hymn, but suddenly remembering the little poem he had been reading in the train, he took the cutting from his pocket, and placing it before him on the organ, Sankey lifted his heart in prayer to God that He might give him a suitable melody to sing the words.

I well remember hearing Mr. Sankey relating the story, during his last visit to this country, in the winter of 1898-99. "Laying my hands upon the organ," he said, "I struck the chord of A flat, and began to sing:

> There were ninety and nine that safely lay
> In the shelter of the fold,
> But one was out on the hills away,
> Far off from the gates of gold—
> Away on the mountains wild and bare,
> Away from the tender Shepherd's care.

"Note by note the tune was given, which has not been changed from that day to this. As the singing ceased, a great sigh seemed to go up from the meeting, and I knew that the song had reached the hearts of my Scottish audience. Mr. Moody was greatly moved. Leaving the pulpit, he came over to where I was seated. Leaning over the organ, he looked at the little newspaper slip from which the song had been sung, and with tears in his eyes, said: 'Sankey, where did you get that hymn? I never heard the like of it in my life.' I was also moved to tears and arose and replied: 'Mr. Moody, that's the hymn I read to you yesterday on the train, which you did not hear.' Then Mr. Moody raised his hand and pronounced the benediction, and the meeting closed. Thus 'The Ninety and Nine' was born."

Miss Clephane was born in Edinburgh, on June 18th, 1830, and when quite young was taken by her parents to reside at Melrose, where she spent

THE NINETY AND NINE

ELIZABETH C. CLEPHANE   IRA D. SANKEY

1. There were ninety and nine that safe - ly lay   In the shel-ter of the
2. "Lord, Thou hast here Thy nine-ty and nine;   Are they not enough,
3. But none of the ransomed ev - er knew   How deep were the w
4. "Lord, whence are those blood-drops all the way That mark out the mo
5. But all thro' the mountains, thun-der-riv'n,   And up from the r

Far off

found my sheep!" And the an - gels 'ech-oed a - round the throne, "Re-

way from the ten-der Shepherd's care, A-way from the ten - der Shep-herd's care
go to the des-ert to find my sheep. I go to the des-ert to find my sheep."
Sick and helpless, and ready to die;   Sick and helpless, and ready to die.
pierced to night by many a thorn;   They're pierced to-night by man y a thorn."
joice, for the Lord brings back His own! Re-joice, for the Lord brings back His own."

BRIDGEND HOUSE.

Where Miss Clephane wrote "The ninety and nine."

the remainder of her life. It was at the place which is still known as Bridge End House that "The Ninety and Nine" was written, about the year 1868—just one year before the death of the author.

Miss Clephane also wrote a few other hymns, including:

> Beneath the Cross of Jesus
> I fain would take my stand,
> The shadow of a mighty Rock
> Within a weary land;
> A home within the wilderness,
> A rest upon the way,
> From the burning of the noontide heat
> And the burden of the day.

HANNAH K. BURLINGHAM.

> I'm waiting for Thee, Lord,
> Thy beauty to see, Lord,
> I'm waiting for Thee, for Thy coming again.
> Thou'rt gone over there, Lord,
> A place to prepare, Lord,
> Thy home I shall share at Thy coming again.

AT the first note of this inspiring Advent hymn, the soul of the singer cannot but be thrilled with joyous anticipation, as, with heart and voice attuned to the heavenly lay, there comes to the waiting one, a longing for the realization of that blessed hope, so eloquently expressed in these sublime lines.

Miss Hannah Kilham Burlingham, the writer of this hymn, was the daughter of Quaker parents, and was born at Evesham, Worcestershire, in 1842. Reared in an atmosphere where the Word of God was read and studied with true piety and reverence, the girl very soon was drawn to the Saviour, realizing that her eternal peace was not to be obtained by her good life and Godly upbringing, but solely through the merits of the atoning blood of the Saviour.

At school Hannah wrote her first poem, for which she was awarded a prize. This was to be the forerunner of many songful lays from her pen. When Miss Burlingham was in her early twenties she withdrew from the Quakers and sought fellowship with Brethren, whose unostentatious form of worship and faithful adherence to New Testament teaching she was led to see, through a diligent study of the Scriptures, was clearly according to the will of God.

It was about this time that Miss Burlingham began writing hymns, many of her first compositions appearing in the "British Herald," a monthly periodical edited by William Reid. They were afterwards reproduced in Reid's "Praise Book," a notable collection, published in 1872, which had a wide circulation.

A true poet, she was passionately fond of music, but as this useful acquirement was rarely encouraged in Quaker homes in those days, there had been scant opportunity for the exercise and development of what musical gift she may have possessed. It was, however, as a hymnwriter and not as a musician that God had marked out H. K. Burlingham for special ministry.

Amongst Brethren, possibly her best loved hymn is "I'm waiting for Thee, Lord," which is frequently sung to the tune originally composed for "When He cometh." North of the Tweed, a favourite melody, and one which exactly suits this easy flowing measure is the plaintive Scottish air "The Land o' the Leal."

Another hymn by the same author which is also a favourite, begins:

> O God of matchless grace,
>   We sing unto Thy name!
> We stand accepted in the place
>   That none but Christ can claim;
> Our willing hearts have heard Thy voice,
> And in Thy mercy we rejoice.

Others familiar to the reader, to be found in the various Brethren hymnals include: "Heirs of Salvation," "Bright, bright home," "The Glory shines before me," and that stirring song of praise—

> Jesus Christ Thou King of Glory,
>   Born a Saviour-Prince to be.

Besides her original compositions Miss Burlingham is also the author of many beautiful translations from the German.

She had the pen of a ready writer, and during her lifetime many of her hymns and poems appeared in various periodicals and hymn books, yet she could never be prevailed upon to publish her writings in book form, and it was not until after her home-call, which came on May 15th, 1901, that some of her best known compositions were issued under the title of "Wayside Songs." A beautiful tribute is paid to the memory of Miss Burlingham by one who knew her intimately: "I never met one who loved her Bible as she did. Though she was interested in current topics, they were wholly subservient to her one great interest. Her love for her Lord and Saviour was deep and real, and one felt, that with her, everything else must take a back place."

FRANCES BEVAN.

ANOTHER lady writer living about this time, whose translations and original compositions occupy a notable position in our hymnody, gave to us that exquisite hymn commencing:

> 'Midst the darkness, storm, and sorrow,
>   One bright gleam I see;
> Well I know the blessed morrow
>   Christ will come for me.
> 'Midst the light, and peace, and glory,
>   Of the Father's home,
> Christ for me is waiting, watching,
>   Waiting till I come.

The name of the author is Mrs. Emma Frances Bevan. She was the daughter of Philip Nicholas Shuttleworth, some time Bishop of Chichester, and was born at Oxford on September 25th, 1827.

Though brought up under the influence of "high church" principles which she early imbibed, Frances Shuttleworth, a few years after the death of her father—which occurred when she was only seventeen—was led to take her place amongst those believers who met on the first day of the week to remember our Saviour's dying love in "the breaking of bread." This came about through attending Bible readings held in the house of a friend, to which the young woman had been invited. It was here that she saw for the first time these truths which eventually led her into the paths of true discipleship.

At the age of twenty-nine she was married to Robert C. L. Bevan, of the noted Lombard Street banking firm, who was well-known for his benevolence and untiring devotion to the Lord's work. Years after, when writing the biography of her husband, Mrs. Bevan tells the story of how

HYMNS AND THEIR WRITERS.

she came to the house of Mr. Bevan to his Bible readings, which were to be the means of leading her into "newness of life." Then Mrs. Bevan reveals to the reader: "As time passed on, I was no more a visitor, but at home in his house."

In the "Believers Hymn Book" the familiar martial air assigned to "Midst the darkness, storm and sorrow" rather detracts from the spirit of the hymn. A more appropriate melody, and one which exactly suits the theme of the song, is the tune set to the hymn in Sankey's hymn book, "Precious thought my Father knoweth." Mrs. Bevan wrote this hymn whilst residing at Princes Gate, London. Much doubt has from time to time arisen as to the authorship of the hymns of this gifted writer because of the fact that when sending each composition forth, instead of placing her own name or initials to it, Mrs. Bevan invariably used the initials of the name of the house where the hymn was written. This has occasioned much perplexity to hymnal editors, as nearly a score of her compositions have different initials affixed to them. For instance, the hymn just referred to bore the initials P. G. ("Princes Gate.").

Frances Bevan wrote a considerable number of original hymns and has published several volumes of poems, but her name, in the realm of hymnody, is best remembered by her excellent translations from the German. Notably amongst these is the well known Gospel hymn from Neumeister (1671-1756).

> Sinners Jesus will receive;
> Sound this word of grace to all
> Who the heavenly pathway leave,
> All who linger, all who fall.

Mrs. Bevan spent the greater part of the later

years of her life along with her husband at Cannes, in the South of France, returning to England during the summer months. When her husband died in 1890, Mrs. Bevan did not again visit England, but continued to reside at Cannes in her house, Chalet Passiflora—which became the birthplace of many of her hymns—where she passed away on February 13th, 1909, in her eighty-second year.

And now to the patient reader who has accompanied me along the pleasant bypaths of hymnody, one word more. It may have been observed that our particular sphere has in a measure been somewhat limited, inasmuch as only the hymns of our assemblies have engaged our particular attention. The mention of these, with their many associations, may have awakened cherished memories, as well as having afforded some pleasurable hours to the spiritual uplifting and edification of those who have accompanied me in our wanderings. It is my sincere hope that the reader may be better able to appreciate the hymns we sing, when we know their story. During our sojourn I have made many friends. We have wandered together through the fragrant meadows of song, our melodious hearts singing in unison the praises of Him, the source of all our song. Thus shall we sing "till some sweet day," when, responsive to the summons of our Lord and Saviour, we shall rise to join the everlasting song in the heavenly courts above. Then:

> O the blessed joy of meeting,
>   All the desert past!
> O the wondrous words of greeting
>   He shall speak at last!
> He and I together entering
>   Those bright courts above;
> He and I together sharing
>   All the Father's love.

Index of Hymns and Authors.

A pilgrim through this lonely world—(Denny)	15
A little while! our Lord shall come—(Deck)	22
Awake, my soul, in joyful lays—(Medley)	25
Alas! and did my Saviour bleed?—(Watts)	32
According to Thy gracious word—(Montgomery)	53
A few more years shall roll—(Bonar)	85
Abide with me—(Lyte)	100, 101
As sinners saved we gladly praise (Evans)	118
Almost persuaded—(Bliss)	148
Around Thy table, holy Lord—(Peters)	192
Behold the Lamb with glory crowned—(Kelly)	12
Bright with all His crowns of glory—(Denny)	15
Bride of the Lamb, rejoice—(Denny)	15
Begone, unbelief! my Saviour is near—(Newton)	43
Behold the throne of grace!—(Newton)	44
Brethren let us join to bless—(Cennick)	69
Be present at our table, Lord—(Cennick)	70
Blessed be God our God—(Bonar)	85
Behold what manner of love—(Sullivan)	157
Beulah Land—(Stites)	166
Before the throne of God above—(Bancroft)	205
Beneath the Cross of Jesus—(Clephane)	207
Bright, bright home—(Burlingham)	209
Come, let us sing the matchless worth—(Medley)	26
Come, Thou Fount of every blessing—(Robinson)	27
Come, let us join our cheerful songs—(Watts)	32
Come, Holy Spirit come—(Hart)	64
Come, ye sinners, poor and wretched—(Hart)	64
Come, weary, anxious, laden soul—(Midlane)	106
Come ye that know the Saviour's name—(Burder)	133
Come, all ye saints of God!—(Boden)	136
Come believing—(Whittle)	155
Come sing, my soul—(Whittle)	155
Crowned with thorns upon the tree—(Guinness)	158
Christians, go and tell of Jesus—(Hammond)	170
Done is the work that saves—(Bonar)	85
Eternal light, eternal light—(Binnie)	105
For ever with the Lord—(Montgomery)	24, 53
From Greenland's icy mountains—(Heber)	32, 102, 161
From every stormy wind that blows—(Stowell)	75, 76
Father! we, Thy children, bless Thee—(Tregelles)	79
For the bread and for the wine—(Bonar)	85
Faint not Christian—(Evans)	119
Fear not children—(Evans)	119
Free from the law—(Bliss)	148
Follow on—(Cushing)	165
Father of mercies!—(Steele)	183
Father, whate'er of earthly bliss—(Steele)	185
Grace 'tis a charming sound—(Doddridge)	24, 46
God moves in a mysterious way—(Cowper)	39, 40
Great Shepherd of Thy chosen flock—(Newton)	45
Guide me, O Thou great Jehovah—(Williams)	49
God's almighty arms are round me—(Denham Smith)	93
God bless our Sunday School—(Midlane)	105
Great the joy where Christians meet!—(Burder)	134
Hark! ten thousand voices crying—(Darby)	20
How sweet the name of Jesus sounds—(Newton)	24, 39, 42, 123
Hark, my soul! it is the Lord—(Cowper)	41
Hail, Thou once despisèd Jesus—(Bakewell)	55

Index of Hymns and Authors.—Continued.

He tenderly binds up the broken in heart—(McCheyne)	60
How good is the God we adore—(Hart)	63
Holy Saviour! we adore Thee—(Tregelles)	77
Here, O my Lord, I see Thee face to face—(Bonar)	85
How vast, how full, how free—(Midlane)	106
How firm a foundation—(Keith)	128
He is my Sun, though He forbear to shine—(Boden)	136
Hold the fort—(Bliss)	148
How beautiful the Saviour's feet—(Guinness)	161
Hiding in Thee—(Cushing)	164, 165
He leadeth me—(Gilmore)	167, 168
He lives—the great Redeemer lives—(Steele)	185
Have ye counted the cost?—(Leeson)	201
Heirs of salvation—(Burlingham)	209
I once was a stranger to grace and to God—(McCheyne)	59
I am a debtor—(McCheyne)	62
I've found the precious Christ of God—(Mason)	70
I'm but a stranger here—(Taylor)	80
I heard the voice of Jesus say—(Bonar)	82, 85
I lay my sins on Jesus—(Bonar)	83, 85
I was a wandering sheep—(Bonar)	85
I am waiting for the dawning—(Francis)	94
I've found a Friend—(Small)	111
I need Thee precious Saviour—(Whitfield)	124
I feel like singing all the time—(Hammond)	143, 171
I'm trusting, I'm trusting—(Russell)	146
I am so glad that Jesus loves me—(Bliss)	148
I will sing of my Redeemer—(Bliss)	150
It is well with my soul—(Spafford)	152
I know whom I have believed—(Whittle)	155
I looked to Jesus—(Whittle)	155
I gave my life for thee—(Havergal)	173
I am Thine, O Lord!—(Crosby)	176
I shall know Him—(Crosby)	178
I have Christ—what want I more—(Walker)	181
I journey through a desert drear—(Walker)	181
I've found a joy in sorrow—(Crewdson)	194
It passeth knowledge—(Shekleton)	195
I'm waiting for Thee, Lord—(Burlingham)	207
Jesus I will trust Thee—(Walker)	23, 181
Join all the glorious names—(Watts)	32
Jesus shall reign—(Watts)	32
Jesus, Lover of my soul—(Wesley)	36, 37, 38, 55
Jehovah Tsidkenu—(McCheyne)	60
Jesus is our Shepherd—(Stowell)	76
Jesus in His heavenly temple—(Chapman)	89
Just as thou are—(Denham Smith)	92
Jesus, Source of life eternal—(Homburg)	120
Jesus! the very thought of Thee—(Bernard of Clairvaux)	123
Jesus is coming—(Whittle)	155
Jesus knows thy sorrow—(Cushing)	165
Just as I am—(Elliott)	181, 186
Look, ye saints, the sight is glorious—(Kelly)	11
Lord Jesus! are we one with Thee?—(Deck)	21
Lamb of God! our souls adore Thee—(Deck)	22
Lord we would ne'er forget Thy love—(Deck)	23
Let us love, and sing, and wonder!—(Newton)	45
Let us rejoice in Christ our Lord—(Newton)	45
Lord, dismiss us with Thy blessing—(Hawker)	65, 66
Lord, dismiss us with Thy blessing—(Fawcett)	67
Lord Jesus, we believing—(Tregelles)	79
Late, late, so late, and dark the night and chill—(Tennyson)	84
Light of the world—(Ed. Bickersteth)	98
Lord Jesus Thine—(Midlane)	106
Lord Jesus Christ we seek Thy face—(Stewart)	110
Lord Jesus, who did'st once appear—(Berridge)	129
Lord Jesus, let Thy favour rest—(Withy)	132
Look unto Me, and be ye saved—(Mackay)	142
Love, deep and strong—(Russell)	147
Low in the grave He lay—(Lowry)	168
Lord, speak to me, that I may speak—(Havergal)	175
Lord! to Thee my heart ascending—(Codner)	189

Index of Hymns and Authors.—Continued.

Loving Shepherd of Thy sheep—(Leeson)	201
May the grace of Christ our Saviour—(Newton)	45
My God, I have found—(Denham Smith)	90
My rest is in heaven—(Lyte)	100
Mid the splendours of the glory—(Reid)	137
Man of Sorrows! what a name—(Bliss)	148, 151
My hope is built on nothing less—(Mote)	161
My God, my Father, while I stray—(Elliott)	187
My chains are snapt—(Carson)	188
'Midst the darkness, storm, and sorrow—(Bevan)	210
Now in a song of grateful praise—(Medley)	24
Not all the blood of beasts—(Watts)	31
No blood, no altar now—(Bonar)	85
No bone of Thee was broken—(Chapman)	89
No condemnation! O my soul—(Chapman)	89
O what a lonely path were ours—(Denny)	15
O Lord, Thy love's unbounded—(Darby)	17
O Lamb of God still keep me—(Deck)	22
O Lord, when we Thy path retrace—(Deck)	22
O happy day when first we felt—(Deck)	22
On Christ salvation rests secure—(Medley)	26
O God, our help in ages past—(Watts)	30
O for a closer walk with God—(Cowper)	41
O happy day that fixed my choice—(Doddridge)	48
O God of Bethel, by whose hand—(Doddridge)	48
Oil for the lamp—(McCheyne)	61
Once more before we part—(Hawker)	65
Onward Christian soldiers—(Baring Gould)	65
Our Saviour crucified—(Chapman)	86
O the deep, deep love of Jesus—(Francis)	97
O Lamb of God! we lift our eyes—(Stewart)	108
O for the robes of whiteness—(Bancroft)	204
O God of matchless grace—(Burlingham)	209
O Love, that wilt not let me go—(Matheson)	113
O how the thought that I should know—(Swain)	121
O, patient, spotless One!—(Bernstein)	125
O teach us more of Thy blest ways—(Hutton)	126
Ours are peace and joy divine—(Reid)	139
On Christ the solid rock I stand—(Mote)	146, 162
Our Lord is now rejected—(Whittle)	153
Oh, what a Saviour, that He died for me—(McGranahan)	156
Oh, safe to the Rock that is higher than I—(Cushing)	164
O spotless Lamb of God, in Thee—(Walker)	180
O Lord, how much Thy name unfolds—(Peters)	192
O blessed Lord what hast Thou done—(Peters)	193
O for the peace that floweth as a river—(Crewdson)	194
O Saviour I have nought to plead—(Crewdson)	194
O Thou whose bounty fills our cup—(Crewdson)	195
O, Christ He is the Fountain—(Cousin)	196
O, Christ what burdens bowed Thy head—(Cousin)	199
One there is above all others—(Nunn)	200
Praise the Saviour, ye who know Him—(Kelly)	9
Praise the Lord who died to save us—(Kelly)	11
Poor, weak, and worthless though I am—(Newton)	45
Prayer is the Soul's sincere desire—(Montgomery)	51
Praise God from whom all blessings flow—(Mason)	70
Peace, perfect peace—(Bickersteth)	99
Passing onward, quickly passing—(Midlane)	106
Praise Him! Praise Him!—(Crosby)	179
Praise ye the Lord, again, again—(Peters)	193
Praise ye Jehovah!—(Campbell)	203
Rise, my soul, Thy God directs thee—(Darby)	20
Rock of ages—(Toplady)	34, 55, 164
Rise, my soul! behold 'tis Jesus—(Denham Smith)	93
Revive Thy work, O Lord!—(Midlane)	104
Ring the bells of heaven—(Cushing)	165
Sweet feast of love Divine—(Denny)	13
Sweeter sound than music knows—(Newton)	45
Sweet the moments rich in blessing—(Shirley)	68
Saviour, we remember Thee!—(Francis)	95
Since Jesus freely did appear—(Berridge)	131
Simply trusting every day—(Stites)	165

Index of Hymns and Authors.—Continued.

Shall we gather at the river—(Lowry)	169, 170
Safe in the arms of Jesus—(Crosby)	177, 179
Saviour, more than life to me—(Crosby)	177
Saved by grace—(Crosby)	178
Sinners Jesus will receive—(Bevan, trans.)	211
The atoning work is done—(Kelly)	12
The head that once was crowned with thorns—(Kelly)	12
To Calvary, Lord! in spirit now—(Denny)	14
'Tis past the dark and dreary night—(Denny)	15
This world is a wilderness wide—(Darby)	19
The veil is rent! Lo, Jesus stands—(Deck)	22
The Saviour lives, no more to die—(Medley)	26
There is a fountain filled with blood—(Cowper)	38
The God of Abraham praise—(Olivers)	56, 57
Ten virgins clothed in white—(McCheyne)	62
This God is the God we adore—(Hart)	64
Thy Name we bless, Lord Jesus!—(Tregelles)	78
Thy broken body, gracious Lord—(Tregelles)	79
The morning, the bright and beautiful morning—(Bonar)	83
Thy way not mine, O Lord—(Bonar)	85
The Lord of Glory! Who is He?—(Chapman)	89
The glory shines before me—(Burlingham)	209
The love that Jesus had for me—(Hall)	202
There is life for a look—(Hall)	202
The Lamb of God to slaughter led—(Chapman)	89
Till He come!—(Bickersteth)	98
There's a Friend for little children—(Midlane)	106, 107
There is a Name I love to hear—(Whitfield)	123
Teach me yet more of Thy blest ways—(Hutton)	127
The crowning day is coming—(Whittle)	155, 157
There shall be showers of blessing—(Whittle)	155, 157
Thou art my joy, Lord Jesus—(Guinness)	161
Thou art the Everlasting Word—(Conder)	115
Thou art coming, O my Saviour—(Havergal)	172
Take my life and let it be—(Havergal)	174
There's a cry from Macedonia—(Crosby)	177
Thou my everlasting portion—(Crosby)	179
Take the world but give me Jesus—(Crosby)	179
'Tis the blessed hour of prayer—(Crosby)	179
The wandered no more will roam—(Walker)	180
Thy gracious presence, O our God—(Steele)	185
The holiest now we enter—(Peters)	193
Through the love of God our Saviour—(Peters)	193
The sands of time are sinking—(Cousin)	197, 198
The ninety and nine—(Clephane)	206
Unto the Lamb that once was slain—(Watts)	32
We'll sing of the Shepherd that died—(Kelly)	11
What grace, O Lord, and beauty shone—(Denny)	15
While in sweet communion feeding—(Denny)	15
When I survey the wonderous Cross—(Watts)	29
With joy we meditate the grace—(Watts)	32
When this passing world is done—(McCheyne)	63
When my Jesus I'm possessing—(Allen)	68
What a Friend we have in Jesus—(Scriven)	72, 73
When the weary, seeking rest—(Bonar)	85
With Jesus in our midst—(Chapman)	88
Without a cloud between—(Midlane)	106
Walk in the light—(Barton)	117
What will it be to dwell above—(Swain)	122
Where shall the weary turn for rest—(Withy)	132
We praise Thee, O God—(Mackay)	140
Worthy, worthy is the Lamb—(Mackay)	142
Worthy, worthy, worthy, Thou of adoration—(Russell)	143
Whosoever will—(Bliss)	148
When peace, like a river—(Spafford)	151
When He cometh—(Cushing)	165
Where is my boy to-night?—(Lowry)	169
What can wash away my stain?—(Lowry)	169
When I survey life's varied scenes—(Steele)	184
When we reach our peaceful dwelling—(Cousin)	199
Yet there is room—(Bonar)	85
Yes, Thou art mine—(Guinness)	161